Summer Bridge Activities ™

creation and design:
Michele D. Van Leeuwen
Scott Van Leeuwen

exercise illustrations by:
Amanda Sorensen

Fourth Grade to Fifth Grade

written by:
Julia Ann Hobbs
Carla Dawn Fisher

Summer Bridge Activities Contains:

Fun, skill-based activities in **reading, writing, arithmetic,** and **language arts** with additional activities in **geography** and **science** to keep your child busy, happy, and learning! SBA is divided into three sections for review and preview with pages numbered by day. Children complete their work quickly with the easy-to-use format, leaving lots of time for play!

A **Reading Book List** based on the Accelerated Reader Program.

Incentive Contracts to encourage summer learning and reward your child's efforts. **"Discover Something New"** lists of creative things to do are found on the backside of each SBA Incentive Contract Calendar for when your child says the inevitable: "What can I do? I'm bored."

Comprehensive **Word Lists,** which contain words to sound, read and spell, challenge children and encourage them to build their vocabulary. SBA 4-5 also contains **Division and Multiplication Flashcards.**

Tear-out answer pages to help correct your child's work.

An official **Certificate of Completion** to be awarded for successfully completing the workbook.

Mr. Fredrickson

Here are some groups who think our books are great!

Ms. Hansen

Hey Kids and Parents!
Log online to summerbrains.com for more eye-boggling, mind-bending, brain-twisting summer fun... it's where summerbrains like you hang out!

www.summerbrains.com

Summer Bridge Activities™
4th to 5th Grade

For information, write:
Rainbow Bridge Publishing, Inc.
332 West Martin Lane, PO Box 571470
Salt Lake City, Utah 84157-1470
801/268-8887
www.rbpbooks.com

Publisher:
Scott G. Van Leeuwen

Associate Publisher:
George Starks

Director of Product Development and Technology:
Dante J. Orazzi

Copy Editors and/or Proofreaders:
Kathleen Bratcher, Suzie Ellison, Jerold Johnson, Randy Harward, Kirsten Swinyard, and Michele Van Leeuwen

Graphic Design and Layout:
Andy Carlson, Dante Orazzi, Amanda Sorensen, Charles Whitehead, and Jeffrey Whitehead

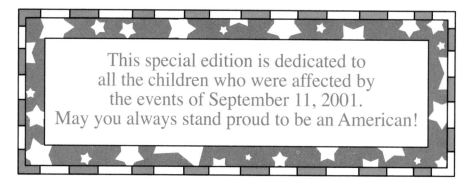

This special edition is dedicated to
all the children who were affected by
the events of September 11, 2001.
May you always stand proud to be an American!

Printed in the U.S.A.

Please visit our website at
www.rbpbooks.com
for supplements, additions, and corrections to this book.

Eighth Edition 2001

For orders call 1-800-598-1441
Discounts available for quantity orders

ISBN: 1-887923-00-4

PRINTED IN THE UNITED STATES OF AMERICA
10 9 8 7 6 5 4 3 2 1

Table of Contents

Dear Parents,

Thank you for choosing Summer Bridge Activities™ to help reinforce your child's classroom skills while away from school. This year, I am proud to offer you this special edition, "Proud To Be An American" to help remind us how fortunate we are for all the freedoms that we enjoy as Americans–education being one of them! I hope you enjoy!

Your personal involvement is so important in your child's immediate and long-term academic success. No matter how wonderful your child's classroom experience is, your involvement outside the classroom will make it that much better!

I originally created Summer Bridge Activities™ because as a parent of a first grader, summer was quickly approaching and I was concerned that the skills he had worked so hard to develop would be forgotten. I was apprehensive about his adjustment to school after three months of play, and wanted to help in any way I could. I spoke with his teacher, other school administrators, and parents, and found I was not alone with my concerns. I was told by several educators that up to 80% of what children are taught in school can be lost, unless that knowledge is reinforced quickly and continuously! I certainly did not want this to happen to my son!

I looked for appropriate workbooks, but could not find any that compare with the Department of Education curriculum guidelines and included all the basic skills in an easy-to-use format. So, as a concerned parent, I organized a team of award-winning teachers and informed educators to create a series of workbooks that would make reviewing classroom skills, including reading, writing, arithmetic, geography, and language arts fun and rewarding. The end result was the Summer Bridge Activities™ workbook that you have in your hands right now! I am confident that you will enjoy using it with your child!

Thanks again for choosing this wonderful program to assist with your child's academic success. I wish you the best of luck in helping your child get the most out of his/her education. Also, we at RBP welcome you to **www.summerbrains.com** where you will find additional fun interactive learning games, ideas, and activities for you and your child at no additional cost! We look forward to seeing you there! Have a great summer and happy learning!

Sincerely,

Michele D. Van Leeuwen

Michele D. Van Leeuwen
Creator of Summer Bridge Activities™

Ms. Hansen TAKES YOU INSIDE Summer Bridge Activities™

The exercises that are found in Summer Bridge Activities™ are easy to understand and are presented in a way that allows your child to review familiar skills and then progressively challenges them on more difficult levels. In addition to academic exercises, Summer Bridge Activities™ contains many other activities to challenge and reinforce reading comprehension, and phonemic awareness.

Sections of Summer Bridge Activities™

 There are three sections to Summer Bridge Activities™; the first and second sections review, the third previews.

 Each section begins with an SBA Incentive Contract Calendar.

 Each day your child will complete an activity in reading, writing, arithmetic, and language skills. The activities progressively become more challenging.

 Each page is numbered by day.

Your child will need a pencil, ruler, eraser, and crayons to complete the activities.

Books Children Love to Read

 SBA contains a Reading Book List with a variety of titles, including many that are found in the Accelerated Reader Program.

 RBP recommends that parents read to their Pre-Kindergarten and Kindergarten-1st Grade children 5-10 minutes each day and then ask questions about the story to reinforce comprehension. For higher grade levels, RBP recommends the following daily reading times: Grades 1–2, 10-20 minutes; Grades 2–3, 20-30 minutes; Grades 3–4, 30-45 minutes; Grades 4-5 and 5-6, 45-60 minutes.

 It is important that the parent and child decide an amount of reading time and write it on the SBA Incentive Contract Calendar.

SBA Incentive Contract Calendars

Calendars are located at the beginning of each section.

We suggest that the parent and child sign the SBA Incentive Contract Calendar before the child begins each section.

When your child completes one day of Summer Bridge Activities™, he/she may color or initial the pencil.

Refer to the recommended reading times. When your child completes the agreed reading time each day, he/she may color or initial the book.

The parent may initial the SBA Incentive Contract Calendar once the activities have been completed.

Let your child explore and experiment with the "Discover Something New" activities found on the back of each SBA Incentive Contract Calendar.

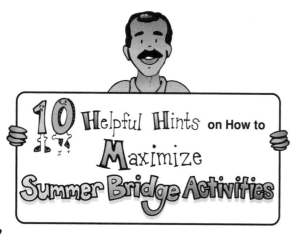

 First, let your child explore the book. Flip through the pages and look at the activities with your child to help him/her become familiar with the book.

 Help select a good time for reading or working on the activities. Suggest a time before your child has played outside and becomes too tired to do their work.

 Provide any necessary materials. A pencil, ruler, eraser, and crayons are all that are required.

 Offer positive guidance. Children need a great deal of guidance. Remember, the activities are not meant to be tests. You want to create a relaxed and positive attitude toward learning. Work through at least one example on each page with your child. "Think aloud" and show your child how to solve problems.

 Give your child plenty of time to think. You may be surprised by how much children can do on their own.

 Stretch your child's thinking beyond the page. If you are reading a storybook, you might ask, "What do you think will happen next?" or "What would you do if this happened to you?" Encourage your child to name objects that begin with certain letters, or count the number of items in your shopping cart. Also, children often enjoy making up their own stories with illustrations.

 Reread stories and occasionally flip through completed pages. Completed pages and books will be a source of pride to your child and will help show how much he/she accomplished over the summer.

 Read and work on activities while outside. Take the workbook out in the back yard, to the park, or to a family camp out. It can be fun wherever you are!

 Encourage siblings, babysitters, and neighborhood children to help with reading and activities. Other children are often perfect for providing the one-on-one attention necessary to reinforce reading skills.

 Give plenty of approval! Stickers and stamps, or even a hand-drawn funny face are effective for recognizing a job well done. When your child completes their book, hang his/her Certificate of Completion where everyone can see it. At the end of the summer, your child can feel proud of his/her accomplishments and will be eager for school to start.

words to
SOUND, READ,
and S-P-E-L-L

At the end of each section are words to sound out, read, and spell.

Together you and your child can:

Write your favorite words on flash cards. Make two sets and play the matching game (in order to keep the two matching cards, you have to know their meaning or spelling).

Draw pictures of exciting words.

Use as many words as you can from the list to make up five questions, statements, or explanations.

Write a story using as many words as you can from the word list.

Write a list of words you find while traveling to the grocery store, on vacation, or on the way to a friend's house.

Write a list of colors.

Write a list of words you have a hard time spelling.

Write a list of action verbs.

Practice writing each word five times.

Reading is the primary means to all learning. If a child cannot read effectively, other classroom subjects can remain out of reach.

You were probably the first person to introduce your child to the wonderful world of reading. As your child grows, it is important to continue encouraging his/her interest in reading to support the skills they are being taught in school.

This summer, make reading a priority in your household. Set aside time each day to read aloud to your child at bedtime or after lunch or dinner. Encourage your child take a break from playing, and stretch out with a book found on the Summer Bridge Activities™ Reading Book List. Choose a title that you have never read, or introduce your child to some of the books you enjoyed when you were their age! Books only seem to get better with time!

Visit the library to find books that meet your child's specific interests. Ask a librarian which books are popular among children of your child's grade. Take advantage of summer storytelling activities at the library. Ask the librarian about other resources, such as stories on cassette, compact disc, and the Internet.

Encourage reading in all settings and daily activities. Encourage your child to read house numbers, street signs, window banners, and packaging labels. Encourage your child to tell stories using pictures.

Best of all, show your child how much YOU like to read! Sit down with your child when he/she reads and enjoy a good book yourself. After dinner, share stories and ideas from newspapers and magazines that might interest your child. Make reading a way of life this summer!

Reading Book List

Sacajawea Books

Hogrogian, Nonny
 Sacajawea
Jassem, Kate
 Sacajawea: Wilderness Guide
Ingoglia, Gina
 Sacajawea and the Journey
  to the Pacific
O'Dell, Scott
 Streams to the River, River to the Sea

Usborne Science Activities

 Science in the Kitchen
 Science with Air
 Science with Batteries
 Science with Light and Mirrors
 Science with Magnets
 Science with Plants
 Science with Weather

Other Great Books

Atwater, Richard
 Mr. Popper's Penguins
Ballard, Robert D.
 Finding the Titanic
Berger, Barbara
 Gwinna
Blume, Judy
 Tales of a Fourth Grade Nothing
 Superfudge
 Fudge-a-mania
Brink, Carol Ryrie
 Caddie Woodlawn
Cleary, Beverly
 Emily's Runaway Imagination
 Henry Huggins
 Mitch and Amy
 Otis Spofford
 Mouse and the Motorcycle
 Socks
 Strider
Clifford, Eth
 Help! I"m a Prisoner in the Library
Cole, Joanna
 The Magic School Bus Books
  At the Waterworks
  Gets Baked in a Cake
  In the Haunted Museum

 Inside the Earth
 Inside the Human Body
 Lost In the Solar System
 Plants Seeds
Coville, Bruce
 My Teacher is an Alien
Dahl, Roald
 Charlie and the Chocolate Factory
 Charlie and the Great Glass Elevator
 Fantastic Mr. Fox
 George's Marvelous Medicine
 Matilda
 The BFG
Dixon, Franklin W.
 Hardy Boys Mysteries
  The Bombay Boomerang
  The Hunting For Hidden Gold
  The Mysterious Caravan
  The Mystery of the Whale Tattoo
  The Pentagon Spy
  The Secret of the Old Mill
  The Shattered Helmet
Doyle, Arthur Conan, Sir
 Sherlock Holmes Mysteries
  Adventure of the Empty House
  Adventures of the Speckled Band
  The Final Problem
Estes, Eleanor Ruth
 The Hundred Dresses
Farley, Walter
 The Black Stallion
 The Black Stallion and Flame
 The Black Stallion and the Girl
 The Black Stallion Challenged
 The Black Stallion Returns
 The Black Stallion's Courage
Feilds, Terri
 Fourth Graders Don't Believe in Witches
Ferguson, Alane
 Cricket and the Crackerbox Kid
Fitzgerald, John Dennis.
 Great Brain books
  Great Brain
  Great Brain at the Academy
  Great Brain Does it Again
  Great Brain Reforms
  More Adventures of the Great Brain
  Return of the Great Brain
Fleischman, Sid
 The Whipping Boy

Gardiner, John R.
Stone Fox
Giff, Patricia R.
Fourth Grade Celebrity
Graham, Kenneth
The Reluctant Dragon
Grove, Vicki
Good-Bye, My Wishing Star
Gurney, James
Dinotopia: A Land Apart from Time
Hass, E. A.
Incognito Mosquito
Incognito Mosquito Flies Again
Incognito Mosquito, Private Insective
Keene, Carolyn
Nancy Drew Mysteries
Case of the Disappearing Diamonds
Clue to the Crumbling Wall
Double Jinx Mystery
Ghost of Blackwood Hall
Secret in the Old Attic
Kingfisher Publications
1,000 Facts about People
1,000 Facts about Earth
1,000 Facts about Wild Animals
Forest Animals
Freshwater Animals
Polar Animals
Kirschner, David
The Pagemaster
Korman, Susan
Alien Alert
Lawson, Robert
Rabbit Hill
Lenski, Lois
Strawberry Girl
Lowry, Lois
All About Sam
Anastasia Krupnik Series
MacDonald, Kate
The Anne of Green Gables Cookbook
MacLachlan, Patricia
Sarah, Plain and Tall
Mills, Lauren A.
The Rag Coat
Morey, Walt
Gentle Ben
Kävik, the Wolf Dog
Mowat, Farley
Owls in the Family
Naylor, Phyllis Reynolds
Shiloh
Paulsen, Gary
Dunc and Amos Hit the Big Top
Dunc's Doll
Dunc's Dump
Hatchet

Rodomonte's Revenge
The Wild Culpepper Cruise
Peet, Bill
Bill Peet: An Autobiography
Sachar, Louis
There's a Boy in the Girls Bathroom
Sideways Stories From Wayside
School
Schulz, Charles
For the Love of Peanuts
King-Smith, Dick
Babe: The Gallant Pig
The Fox Busters
Martin's Mice
Kline, Suzy
Orp
Orp and the Chop Suey Burgers
Orp Goes to the Hoop
Who's Orp's Girlfriend?
Lowry, Lois
Attaboy, Sam!
Manes, Stephanie
Chocolate Covered Ants
Prelutsky, Jack
For Laughing Out Loud: Poems to Tickle
Your Funny Bone
Pryor, Bonnie
Poison Ivy and Eyebrow Wigs
Richler, Mordecia
Jacob Two-Two and the Dinosaur
Jacob Two-Two Meets the Hooded Fang
Rockwell, Thomas
How to Eat Fried Worms
Sachar, Louis
Sideways Arithmetic From Wayside School
Scieszka, Jon
The Good, The Bad, and the Goofy
Knights of the Kitchen Table
Your Mother Was a Neanderthal
Schwartz, Alvin
Scary Stories To Tell in the Dark
Silverstein, Shel
Where the Sidewalk Ends
Titus, Eve
Basil of Baker Street
Wittman, Sally
Stepbrother Sabotage
Wright, Betty
The Ghost of Popcorn Hill

Summer Bridge Activities™
Incentive Contract Calendar

Month _____July_____

My parents and I decided that if I complete 15 days of
Summer Bridge Activities™ and read ____30____ minutes a day,
my incentive/reward will be:

_____

Child's Signature   _____Ashley_____
Parent's Signature   _____

Day 1	📖 ⭐ —		Day 8	📖 ⭐ —	
Day 2	📖 ⭐ —		Day 9	📖 ⭐ —	
Day 3	📖 ⭐ —		Day 10	📖 ⭐ —	
Day 4	📖 ⭐ —		Day 11	📖 ⭐ —	
Day 5	📖 ⭐ —		Day 12	📖 ⭐ —	
Day 6	📖 ⭐ —		Day 13	📖 ⭐ —	
Day 7	📖 ⭐ —		Day 14	📖 ⭐ —	
			Day 15	📖 ⭐ —	

Child: Color the ⭐ for daily activities completed.
Color the 📖 for daily reading completed.

Parent: Initial the ___ for daily activities and reading
your child completes.

Fun Activity Ideas to Go Along with the First Section!

1. Describe what you look like and write it down.

2. Make a picnic lunch for two, then invite a friend over and have a picnic in your backyard.

3. Feed the birds.

4. Ask your mom or dad for an old map and plan a trip. Decide on a destination and highlight your route. Figure out how many days it would take, where would you stop and what you would like to see. Use the legend on the map to help you make these decisions.

5. Find some old socks, buttons, yarn, and needle and thread. Make puppets and name them. Then find a cardboard box and paint it. Cut a hole in the front to put the puppets through, and put on a puppet show for younger children.

6. Polish a pair of your mom's or dad's shoes and put a love note in the toe.

7. Visit a sick neighbor, friend, or relative.

8. Hold a fire drill in your home.

9. Start a diary.

10. Learn how to do something you have always wanted to do, like play the guitar, cross-stitch, rollerblade, cook pizza, train your dog, etc.

11. Write a story about your friend.

12. In the evening, look at the sky. Find the first star and make a wish.

13. Pick one of your favorite foods and learn how to make it.

14. Have a watermelon bust.

15. Make a pitcher of lemonade or tropical Kool-Aid and sell it in front of your house.

Add or subtract these three or four digit numbers.

1. 681
   + 145

2. 569
   - 247

3. 3,744
   - 1,378

4. 8,171
   + 7,445

5. 1,355
   + 1,927

6. 248
   + 48

7. 143
   + 219

8. 2,830
   - 519

9. 9,873
   + 828

10. 5,893
    + 3,072

11. 304
    - 172

12. 4,918
    + 3,928

13. 6,219
    - 4,356

14. 2,456
    + 1,529

15. 1,375
    + 6,518

16. 428
    - 119

17. 2,709
    + 1,282

18. 7,645
    - 564

19. 1,680
    - 354

20. 6,142
    - 2,525

Add the correct word — their or there. Remember: their means "they own" or "have," and there means "in or at the place" or it can begin a sentence.

1. _____ must be something wrong with that cow.
2. The Hills were training _____ horse to jump.
3. We are going to _____ farm tomorrow.
4. Please put the boxes over _____.
5. _____ will be sixteen people at the party.
6. Will you please sit here, not _____?
7. _____ barn burned down yesterday.
8. They will put _____ animals in Mr. Jack's barn tonight.

Write four sentences about your school. Use their in two of them and there in the other two.

9. _____
10. _____
11. _____
12. _____

Day 2

Suffixes. A suffix is a syllable added to the end of a base word. Add the suffix in the middle of the suffix wheel to the end of the base word. Write the new word. <u>Remember</u>: You may need to double the final consonant or change a (y) to an (i) when adding a suffix.

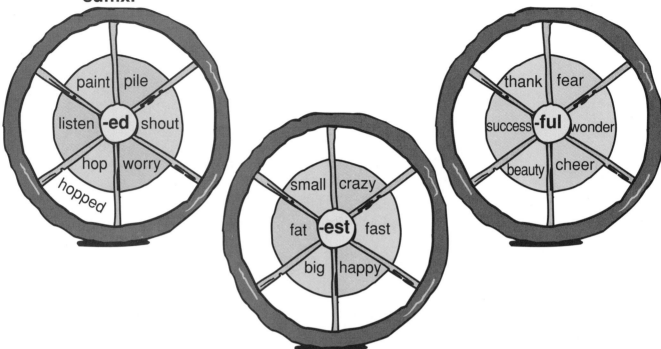

Producers and Consumers. Write answers to the following questions or discuss them with an adult.

1. Name some producers. _____

_____

2. How are producers and consumers different? _____

_____

3. What does profit, labor, and wages have to do with producers and consumers?

_____

4. How are producers and consumers interdependent? _____

_____

5. Must people buy what they need or want from other people? _____

_____

6. How do you think consumers and producers of today are different from consumers and producers of years ago? _____

_____

_____

Understanding Thousands. **Write each number in standard form. The first one has been done for you.**

1. 8 thousands, 3 tens, 9 ones

   8,039

2. 1 thousand, 7 tens, 5 ones

   _____

3. 6,000 + 300 + 10 + 2

   _____

4. 2,000 + 900 + 80 + 9

   _____

5. 3 thousands, 8 hundreds, 4 tens, 1 one

   _____

6. 6 thousands, 9 hundreds, 9 tens, 6 ones

   _____

7. 5,000 + 700 + 3

   _____

8. 1,000 + 400 + 10

   _____

9. 7 thousands, 1 hundred, 7 ones

   _____

10. 0 thousands, 4 hundreds, 7 tens

    _____

11. 9,000 + 900 + 90 + 9

    _____

12. 7,000 + 900 + 5

    _____

13. 2 thousands, 9 hundreds, 6 tens, 2 ones

    _____

14. 4 thousands, 5 tens

    _____

15. 1,000 + 8

    _____

16. 3,000 + 10 + 5

    _____

Read the following paragraph and answer the questions.

Kangaroos are furry, hopping mammals that live only in Australia. Antelope kangaroos live on the plains in the north. Gray kangaroos live mostly in the grasslands and forests of eastern and southern Australia. Red kangaroos make their home in the deserts and dry grasslands in the central part of the country, and most wallaroos live in dry, rocky hills.

1. What is the main idea of this paragraph?

   _____

   _____

   _____

2. List some of the important details of the paragraph?

   _____

   _____

   _____

   _____

Products. **What products might we get from the** <u>seven</u> <u>major</u> <u>regions</u> **of our country? See if you can put the correct region next to the correct products.**

- **Great Lakes**
- **Mountain**
- **Southwest**
- **Northeast**
- **Plains**
- **Pacific**
- **Southeast**

_____ 1. The main crops are sugarcane, oranges, soybeans, rice, peanuts, and tobacco. The main minerals are oil, iron ore, limestone, and coal. Hickory, oak, maple, and lots of other trees are used for furniture, paper, and other products.

_____ 2. Lots of different kinds of fish and shellfish are found here: cod, butterfish, clams, lobsters, squid, sea bass, flounder, sole, and swordfish. Farm products include milk, cheese, eggs, fruits, vegetables, chicken, turkey, tomatoes, blueberries, cranberries, maple syrup, and grapes. This region also produces lots of coal.

_____ 3. Record amounts of corn, soybeans, and oats are found here. Other crops include fruits and vegetables. This area is rich in minerals, iron ore, and coal. This area is also rich in dairy products. This is called the "Corn Belt" of the United States.

_____ 4. Corn and wheat grow well here. A lot of farming, ranching, and mining is done here. This area manufactures a lot of hot dogs, flour, and breakfast cereals.

_____ 5. The largest crop in this area is cotton. Other crops are oranges, grapefruit, rice, and wheat. They raise <u>a</u> <u>lot</u> of cattle and sheep here. Silver and copper are found in this region. Fuels are also plentiful, such as coal, natural gas, uranium, and oil.

_____ 6. There is a wide variety of products from this area because of the two very different climate areas. Products include oil, king crab, salmon, timber, as well as pineapple, macadamia nuts, fruits, nuts, berries, and vegetables. This area also produces petroleum and natural gas. It has the <u>top</u> agricultural state in the nation, as well as the top commercial fishing region.

_____ 7. Some of the major minerals found in this region are gold, lead, silver, copper, and zinc. There is also a lot of natural gas, coal, and oil to be found. Wheat, peas, beans, sugar beets, and potatoes are grown here. Ranching includes beef cattle, sheep, and dairy cows.

Estimating Sums and Differences. When estimating numbers, round them off then add or subtract. <u>Remember</u>: answers are not exact.

EXAMPLE: 420 + 384 = 420 is close to <u>400</u> and 384 is close to <u>400</u> so your answer would be <u>800</u> when estimating. **Try estimating these problems!**

1. 88 + 19 = _____   2. 81 + 75 = _____   3. 93 - 85 = _____

4. 98 - 12 = _____   5. 93 - 39 = _____   6. 891 - 551 = _____

7. 57 - 39 = _____   8. 24 + 35 = _____   9. 209 + 179 = _____

10. 64 + 39 = _____   11. 56 - 33 = _____   12. 288 + 398 = _____

13. 78 - 18 = _____   14. 75 - 42 = _____   15. 540 + 317 = _____

16. 66 + 12 = _____   17. 30 + 71 = _____   18. 610 - 273 = _____

19. 63 + 93 = _____   20. 91 + 65 = _____   21. 247 - 210 = _____

Write the five steps to the writing or composition process. Then write a short story of your own. Use all five steps you will need additional paper.

Story: _____

Prefixes. **Prefixes are syllables added to the beginning of a base word. Add a prefix to these base words. The first one has been done for you.**

1. Will you __un__ lock the door?
2. Can you ____call what he said?
3. The genie will ____appear if you clap your hands.
4. Janet will ____fold the napkins.
5. Do you ____agree with what I said?
6. Mother is going to ____arrange the front room.
7. The picture was the shape of a ____angle.
8. Everyone needs to come ____board now.
9. Erin and Eli will ____form in the ballet.
10. You can count on me to ____pay you.
11. Look out for the ____coming traffic!
12. The Damon's have six ____phones in their house.
13. There is a big ____count on the cost of this table.
14. That was a very ____wise thing to do.

Local, State, and Federal Government Activity. **Pick up a telephone directory, then look up and record titles listed under local, state, and federal government. Record some at each level.**

Telephone Directory

Local	Federal	State
_____	_____	_____
_____	_____	_____
_____	_____	_____
_____	_____	_____
_____	_____	_____
_____	_____	_____
_____	_____	_____
_____	_____	_____

Number Families. You can practice basic facts by using "families of facts."

7 + 2 = 9	2 + 7 = 9	9 - 2 = 7	9 - 7 = 2
3 x 6 = 18	6 x 3 = 18	18 ÷ 3 = 6	18 ÷ 6 = 3

Complete the number families below.

1. 9, 7, 16

9 + 7 = 16

___ + ___ = ___

___ - ___ = ___

___ - ___ = ___

2. 3, 9, 27

3 x 9 = 27

___ x ___ = ___

___ ÷ ___ = ___

___ ÷ ___ = ___

3. 4, 8, 32

4 x 8 = 32

___ x ___ = ___

___ ÷ ___ = ___

___ ÷ ___ = ___

4. 8, 5, 40

8 x 5 = 40

___ x ___ = ___

___ ÷ ___ = ___

___ ÷ ___ = ___

5. 3, 8, 11

3 + 8 = 11

___ + ___ = ___

___ - ___ = ___

___ - ___ = ___

6. 3, 4, 12

3 x 4 = 12

___ x ___ = ___

___ ÷ ___ = ___

___ ÷ ___ = ___

7. 12, 11, 23

12 + 11 = 23

___ + ___ = ___

___ - ___ = ___

___ - ___ = ___

8. 612, 208, 820

612 + 208 = 820

___ + ___ = ___

___ - ___ = ___

___ - ___ = ___

Nouns are words that name people, places, or things.
Common nouns name any person, place, or thing.
Proper nouns name a particular person, place, or thing.
Draw a circle around the common nouns and underline the proper nouns in the following sentences. The first one has been done for you.

1. Many (people) like to travel in <u>England</u>.
2. Christopher Columbus was an explorer.
3. Antarctica is a continent.
4. The ships crossed the Atlantic Ocean.
5. We paddled the canoe down the Red River.
6. Astronauts explore space for the United States.
7. San Francisco is the city by the bay.
8. Julie and Ashley visited their aunt in Boston.
9. Mt. Smart is a small mountain in Idaho.
10. Thursday is Andrew's birthday.
11. What state does Mike live in?
12. Are Hilary and her brother going to the circus?
13. Brian went to the library to get some books.

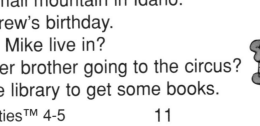

Draw lines between these words and their abbreviations.

EXAMPLE:

Sunday	mag.	dozen	Fri.
magazine	pd.	Friday	tel.
quart	ex.	principal	univ.
November	Sun.	telephone	pt.
paid	oz.	volume	ave.
pages	ft.	pint	Oct.
ounce	Nov.	William	wk.
package	qt.	October	prin.
Doctor	pp.	street	st.
example	govt.	university	Wm.
government	Dr.	week	vol.
foot	pkg.	avenue	doz.

● ●

Our Government. **There are three kinds of government: local, state, and federal (or national). Each kind handles problems of different sizes. They try to solve problems that people cannot solve alone. Put the following statements on problem solving and choices in the correct sequence (1,2,3,4).**

_____ Write down the possible results of each choice, whether it's good or bad.

_____ List all the choices or possibilities there are in connection to the problem or situation.

_____ If there is more than one person involved, or if it involves <u>money</u>, people take a vote.

_____ Decide what is most important and which choice or choices will best solve the problem.

Now choose a problem or choice that you are facing and try to follow some or all of the steps above. This problem or choice may affect just you, or it might affect those around you.

Money Sense.

1. Cammie has 3 coins with a value of 11¢. What are the coins?

_____

2. Janet has 6 coins with the value of 47¢. What are they coins?

_____

3. Frankie has 5 coins that have the value of 17¢. What 5 coins add up to 17¢?

_____

4. Tenley has 7 coins. The value of the coins is 20¢. Find 7 coins with the value of 20¢.

_____

5. Jake has 4 coins. One of them is a quarter. The value of his coins is 45¢. What coins does he have?

_____

_____

6. Gary has 6 coins with a value of 40¢. Find the 6 coins that Gary has with the value of 40¢.

_____

_____

Singular (One) and Plural (More Than One) Nouns. Write the singular or plural form of the following nouns.

EXAMPLE:

bee _____*bees*_____

1. bunny _____
2. cities _____
3. toe _____
4. buses _____
5. branch _____
6. foot _____
7. sheep _____
8. men _____
9. face _____
10. berries _____
11. donkey _____
12. stitch _____
13. oxen _____

EXAMPLE:

boys _____*boy*_____

14. windows _____
15. child _____
16. libraries _____
17. movie _____
18. goose _____
19. deer _____
20. boxes _____
21. class _____
22. woman _____
23. tax _____
24. circuses _____
25. turkeys _____
26. book _____

Which word referent should be used in place of the word or words in parenthesis? Write it in the blank. <u>He, she, you, it, they, him, her, them, then, here, us,</u> and <u>there</u> are all word referents.

Barbara and Denise were best friends. (Barbara and Denise) _____ had decided to go on a trip together this summer. With maps and brochures scattered all over Barbara's floor, (Barbara and Denise) _____ started looking for a place to go. One brochure was telling about an interesting place, (The brochure) _____ was about Yellowstone Park. "Let's go (Yellowstone) _____!" cried Denise. "(Yellowstone) _____ would be a fun place to go. I think we should ask my brother to go with us," said Barbara. "(My brother) _____ could do a lot of the driving for (Barbara and Denise) _____."

Tom's car was packed and ready to go the next morning, (The car) _____ was a new 4x4 Ranger. (Barbara, Denise, and Tom) _____ would have taken Barbara's car but (Barbara's) _____ car had a flat tire.

After driving for two days the travelers got to Yellowstone Park. Tom shouted, "At last we are (at Yellowstone) _____!" (Tom) _____ was tired of driving. (The trip) _____ turned out to be a fun trip for (Denise, Barbara, and Tom) _____.

● ●

Points of Interest. **What makes the state, town, or country that you live in an interesting place? Write a campaign or advertisement to get people to visit or even live in your state, town, or country. What are the points of interest? What makes it special and different from other places?**

_____

_____

_____

_____

_____

_____

Write the number that is <u>10 more</u> than the number and then write the number that is <u>10 less</u> than the number. The first one is done for you.

1. 59	**2.** 496	**3.** 951	**4.** 392
<u>69</u> , <u>49</u>	____ , ____	____ , ____	____ , ____
5. 164	**6.** 703	**7.** 73	**8.** 1,946
____ , ____	____ , ____	____ , ____	____ , ____

Do the same thing as above except use <u>100 more</u> than the number and <u>100 less</u> than the number.

9. 150	**11.** 555	**13.** 871	**15.** 3,102
____ , ____	____ , ____	____ , ____	____ , ____
10. 703	**12.** 493	**14.** 1,956	**16.** 5,691
____ , ____	____ , ____	____ , ____	____ , ____

Write a proper noun for each of the common nouns listed below.
<u>Remember</u>: Proper nouns start with capital letters.

EXAMPLE:

building _White House_

1. National park_____
2. holiday _____
3. dam _____
4. state _____
5. river _____

6. person _____
7. desert _____
8. day _____
9. island_____
10. street_____

Now write a common noun for the following proper nouns.

1. Golden Gate _____
2. San Francisco _____
3. Pacific _____
4. November _____
5. Canada _____

6. Joseph _____
7. Liberty Bell _____
8. <u>Pete's Dragon</u> _____
9. Jupiter _____
10. Indians _____

Father's Day. **Write about fathers, then draw a picture. Fathers should always…. Father should never…. If I were a father I would want to always….**

_____

_____

_____

_____

_____

_____

_____

_____

_____

_____

_____

_____

_____

_____

_____

_____

_____

_____

_____

_____

_____

Draw your picture here!

Adding Thousands. If you have a  use it to check your answers.

1.	2,456 + 1,527	2.	9,873 + 1,828	3.	7,125 + 2,008	4.	4,678 + 3,321

5.	18,086 + 12,302	6.	8,377 + 13,674	7.	10,308 + 23,548	8.	19,873 + 1,828

9.	626 8,024 + 3,643	10.	3,481 309 + 4,877	11.	1,465 388 + 3,035	12.	430 2,824 + 4,099

A singular (one) possessive noun is usually formed by adding -'s — animal's. A plural (two or more) possessive noun is usually formed by adding - s' — animals'. Choose a singular or plural possessive noun to fill in the blanks. Hint: look at the word after the blank to help you decide if it's singular or plural.

Word Box

birds'
woman's
child's
dog's
children's
Rabbits'
cows'
lady's
plumbers'
Ann's

1. The _____ toy is broken.

2. _____ tails are fluffy.

3. My _____ leash is black.

4. After the accident the _____ tools were all over the road.

5. The _____ pets are in a pet show.

6. The _____ coat is made of fur.

7. We hope that _____ picture will win the prize.

8. The _____ mooing was loud and noisy.

9. That _____ hat blew away in the wind storm.

10. The _____ nests were high up in the trees.

Write the contractions to fill in the circles of the puzzle.

1. I would
2. is not
3. they will
4. should have
5. who are
6. these will
7. must not
8. there have
9. need not
10. it had
11. will not
12. what has
13. might have
14. one is

Regions of Our Country. Our country is divided into seven regions. <u>Great Lakes</u>, <u>Plains</u>, <u>Mountain</u>, and <u>Pacific</u> are all regions named after bodies of water or important landforms. The other three major regions, <u>Southwest</u>, <u>Southeast</u>, and <u>Northeast</u>, are named for intermediate directions. Label the seven major regions of our United States.

1. _____
2. _____
3. _____
4. _____
5. _____
6. _____
7. _____

*Something to think about. What about Hawaii and Alaska? What region or immediate direction would they belong to?

Hawaii _____ Alaska _____

Subtracting Thousands. **Check your answers with a calculator if you have one.**

1. 8,425 − 3,519	**2.** 4,888 − 1,777	**3.** 4,314 − 2,532	**4.** 3,826 − 49
5. 9,453 − 3,168	**6.** 5,835 − 1,290	**7.** 2,182 − 396	**8.** 6,922 − 5,833
9. 8,000 − 5,603	**10.** 2,493 − 1,617	**11.** 22,318 − 17,725	**12.** 57,260 − 23,458

Write the singular and plural possessive forms of the following nouns. The first one is done for you.

<u>Singular</u>	<u>Possessive</u>	<u>Plural</u>	<u>Possessive</u>
boy	*boy's*	boys	*boys'*
key	_____	keys	_____
bird	_____	birds	_____
mouse	_____	mice	_____
puppy	_____	puppies	_____
woman	_____	women	_____
class	_____	classes	_____
rollerblade	_____	rollerblades	_____
flag	_____	flags	_____
computer	_____	computers	_____

Cross out the word that does not belong in the sentence.

EXAMPLE: It's great that we ~~us~~ often agree on things.

1. All butterflies will be gone ~~went~~ by October.
2. Idaho ~~are~~ is known as the "Potato State."
3. She will ~~hid~~ hide behind that large old tree.
4. I have ridden ~~rode~~ my horse regularly this summer.
5. Our dog consistently goes to that corner to dig ~~digging~~.
6. My baby sister always drinks ~~dranks~~ her milk.
7. Lee Ann had to ~~swept~~ sweep out the garage.
8. I ~~were~~ was very irritated with my friend.
9. How long have you known ~~know~~ Susan Green?
10. We have ~~has~~ been forbidden to go into the cave.
11. Have you done ~~did~~ your chores?
12. The scared boy ran ~~run~~ all the way home.
13. He has done ~~did~~ well in all sports.
14. The wind has ~~blew~~ blown for five days.

Time Zones. **Unscramble the answers.**

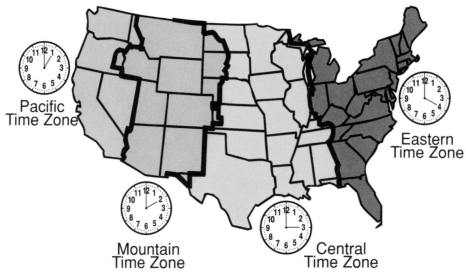

Pacific Time Zone

Eastern Time Zone

Mountain Time Zone

Central Time Zone

1. Time zones are different because of the <u>usn</u>. _____

2. As we go east the time is <u>treal</u>._____

3. As we go west the time is <u>rrilaee</u>. _____

4. You can find time zone maps in a <u>lwdro</u> <u>manaacl</u>. _____

5. If you want to find the time in a certain zone to the east you might want to <u>dad</u> <u>suohr</u> _____ not <u>trtbuacs</u> <u>suohr</u>. _____

6. Remember different parts of the world receive sunlight at different times. That is why, we have different <u>meit</u> <u>sonze</u>. _____

Multiplication. **Find each product.**

EXAMPLE:

1. 9 x 2 = 18
2. 8 x 4 = _____
3. 5 x 6 = _____
4. 7 x 3 = _____
5. 4 x 6 = _____
6. 9 x 5 = _____
7. 8 x 6 = _____
8. 5 x 7 = _____
9. 3 x 9 = _____
10. 7 x 6 = _____
11. 1 x 9 = _____

12. 4 x 7 = _____
13. 8 x 3 = _____
14. 3 x 3 = _____
15. 6 x 3 = _____
16. 6 x 9 = _____
17. 6 x 6 = _____
18. 9 x 4 = _____
19. 7 x 7 = _____
20. 7 x 8 = _____
21. 7 x 9 = _____
22. 9 x 9 = _____

23. 8 x 5 = _____
24. 3 x 4 = _____
25. 5 x 5 = _____
26. 8 x 7 = _____
27. 7 x 3 = _____
28. 8 x 8 = _____
29. 9 x11 = _____
30. 9 x10 = _____
31. 9 x 7 = _____
32. 8 x 9 = _____

Main Verbs and *Helping Verbs.* **Helping verbs help the main verb. The main verb shows action. Underline the main verbs. Circle the helping verbs.**

1. It has been raining for five days.
2. Jack had finished his lessons before 10:00.
3. I have enjoyed the children this month.
4. We were cleaning the house for our friend.
5. The babies have been sleeping for two hours.
6. Two rafts were floating down the river.

Main
Verbs

Helping
Verbs

Fill in the blank with a helping verb.

7. David _____ diving into the pond.
8. The pool _____ _____ used all summer.
9. I _____ waiting for them to fix it.
10. They _____ _____ working on it for three weeks.
11. It _____ _____ fun without the pool.
12. Seven sheep _____ running loose in the street.

The months of the year and the days of the week are written below in order. On the lines below write the months and days in alphabetical order. Write in cursive.

January February March April May June July August September October November December Sunday Monday Tuesday Wednesday Thursday Friday Saturday

1. _____
2. _____
3. _____
4. _____
5. _____
6. _____
7. _____
8. _____
9. _____
10. _____
11. _____
12. _____
13. _____
14. _____
15. _____
16. _____
17. _____
18. _____
19. _____

World Globe. **Read the information given, then label the following.**

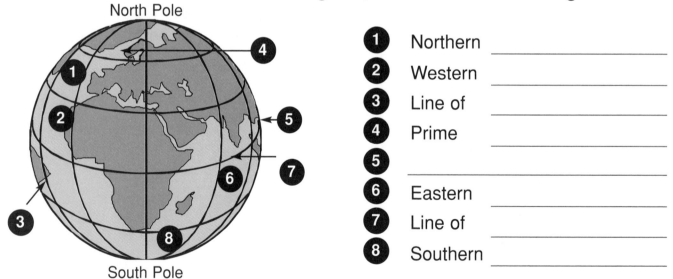

North Pole

South Pole

1. Northern _____
2. Western _____
3. Line of _____
4. Prime _____
5. _____
6. Eastern _____
7. Line of _____
8. Southern _____

We use different terms to locate places on maps and globes. We use lines of <u>latitude</u> to go around the globe from east to west. These lines run parallel to each other, never touching each other. Lines of <u>longitude</u> run north and south on a map or globe and are sometimes called <u>meridians</u>.

The <u>equator</u> is a line of <u>latitude</u> that divides the earth in half running west to east. The top half is called the <u>Northern Hemisphere</u>; the bottom half is called the <u>Southern Hemisphere</u>. The Prime Meridian is a line of <u>longitude</u>. It runs from north to south. So the equator is a line of <u>latitude</u>, and the <u>Prime Meridian</u> is a line of <u>longitude</u>.

Adding or Subtracting Thousands. **Check your answers using a calculator if you have one.**

1. 7,458 − 3,762	2. 8,562 + 2,163	3. 5,585 − 2,609	4. 6,052 − 5,381	5. 7,871 + 1,695
6. 36,814 − 7,523	7. 53,397 + 39,288	8. 19,506 + 34,947	9. 18,103 − 9,079	10. 43,470 − 3,746
11. 3,245 5,029 + 6,981	12. 9,421 8,389 + 4,506	13. 3,340 7,189 + 4,482	14. 46,306 18,782 + 3,115	15. 36,814 17,288 + 29,397

Present tense verbs happen now. Past tense verbs have already happened. Write the past or present tense for these verbs.

EXAMPLE: **stay—present tense; stayed—past tense.**

Present	**Past**		**Present**	**Past**
1. hop	_____	6.	_____	thanked
2. skate	_____	7.	_____	called
3. love	_____	8.	_____	sprained
4. play	_____	9.	_____	wrapped
5. work	_____	10.	_____	hugged

Past Tense With a Helper. Write the past tense.

Present Tense	**Past Tense with Helping Verb**
EXAMPLE:	
1. walk	has, have, had *walked*
2. jog	has, have, had _____
3. hurry	has, have, had _____
4. empty	has, have, had _____
5. chase	has, have, had _____

Continental Congress adopted the first official American flag in Philadelphia, Pennsylvania on June 14, 1777. History tells us that at that particular time the thirteen colonies were fighting for their liberty. The flag was a symbol of unity.
Choose one or more of the following activities.

1. Compare our flag today with the first American flag. Write a short paragraph about it.
2. Write what your life may have been like during that time, compared to what it is now.
3. Find out what the stars, stripes, and colors of the flag stand for, and write a paragraph.

_____
_____
_____
_____
_____
_____
_____
_____
_____
_____
_____

Your Choice of Rooms. **Choose a room in your house and measure the floor space. Measure it in either feet or meters. Draw and label it.**

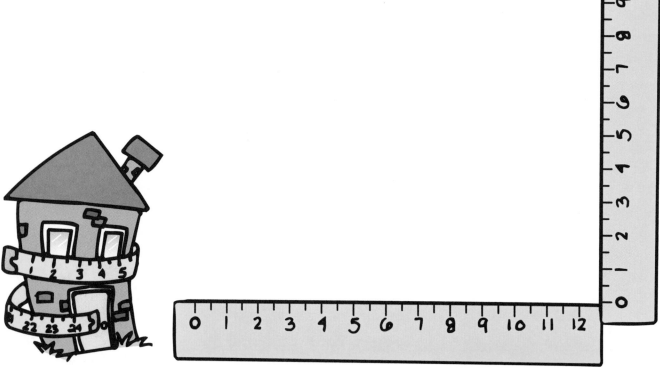

Division. **Find each quotient.**

1. 20 ÷ 4 = _____
2. 28 ÷ 4 = _____
3. 14 ÷ 7 = _____
4. 0 ÷ 2 = _____
5. 42 ÷ 6 = _____
6. 30 ÷ 5 = _____
7. 32 ÷ 4 = _____
8. 25 ÷ 5 = _____
9. 81 ÷ 9 = _____
10. 49 ÷ 7 = _____
11. 18 ÷ 6 = _____
12. 63 ÷ 7 = _____
13. 40 ÷ 5 = _____
14. 36 ÷ 9 = _____
15. 72 ÷ 9 = _____
16. 54 ÷ 6 = _____
17. 48 ÷ 6 = _____
18. 32 ÷ 8 = _____
19. 45 ÷ 9 = _____
20. 36 ÷ 6 = _____
21. 54 ÷ 9 = _____
22. 48 ÷ 8 = _____
23. 63 ÷ 9 = _____
24. 99 ÷ 9 = _____

Fill in the blanks with the past tense. Hint: You will have to change the spelling. The first one is done for you.

Past Tense

1. Bells <u>ring</u>.   Bells ___*rang*___.

2. We <u>eat</u>.   We _____.

3. I <u>wear</u> it.   I _____ it.

4. You <u>make</u> some.   You _____ some.

5. They <u>sing</u>.   They _____.

6. I <u>throw</u>.   I _____.

7. I <u>say</u>.   I _____.

8. They <u>take</u>.   They _____.

Fill in the blank with the past tense of the verb.

9. Sam _____ he wanted to stay in touch with Kit.   (know)

10. Katie _____ a letter to Ron.   (write)

11. He has _____ his friend with him.   (bring)

12. The men have _____ to dig the ditch.   (begin)

13. That little girl has _____ her doll again.   (break)

14. I _____ her new car to the play.   (drive)

Replace the word <u>said</u> in these sentences with another word that fits the meaning.

EXAMPLE:

1. The man (said) _____*yelled*_____, "Get that cat out of here!"

2. Margaret (said) _____, "Please, don't do that."

3. Mother always (said) _____, "A stitch in time saves nine."

4. "This is my country," (said) _____ the man with a tall hat.

5. "Is it time to go home so soon?" (said) _____ Mike.

6. "I don't like vegetables in soups," (said) _____ Dad.

7. "My sore throat still hurts," (said) _____ Nicholas.

8. The weatherman (said) _____ that it will be windy today.

9. The boy with a mouth full of candy (said) _____ he wanted more.

10. I called Megan on the phone, and she (said) _____, "There's no school today."

11. The shopkeeper (said) _____, "Do you want red or orange socks?"

12. Kristine Jones (said) _____ her mother makes the best cookies.

According to the encyclopedia, the sun was born about 4,600,000,000 years ago. What else do you know about the sun? Read and then write some interesting facts about the sun. You may want to write about the things you like to do during hot weather when the sun shines.

_____

_____

_____

_____

_____

_____

_____

_____

_____

Multiplication With Three Factors. **Find the product of the three factors.**

EXAMPLE: **6 x 1 x 3 = 6 x 1 = 6 x 3 = 18**

1. 2 x 4 x 2 = ___   2. 3 x 3 x 5 = ___   3. 4 x 2 x 2 = ___   4. 2 x 5 x 1 = ___

5. 4 x 2 x 4 = ___   6. 2 x 3 x 7 = ___   7. 0 x 9 x 9 = ___   8. 3 x 2 x 3 = ___

9. 3 x 3 x 3 = ___   10. 5 x 2 x 2 = ___   11. 4 x 2 x 5 = ___   12. 2 x 3 x 6 = ___

13. 1 x 2 x 3 = ___   14. 3 x 3 x 0 = ___   15. 3 x 5 x 0 = ___   16. 1 x 3 x 5 = ___

17. 2 x 3 x 4 = ___   18. 2 x 2 x 3 = ___   19. 4 x 3 x 2 = ___   20. 8 x 1 x 8 = ___

21. 3 x 3 x 8 = ___   22. 3 x 5 x 1 = ___   23. 6 x 3 x 1 = ___   24. 4 x 1 x 3 = ___

Write four sentences using the word <u>are</u>. Write four sentences using the word <u>our</u>. The first two are done for you.

1. <u>Our</u> house is almost finished.

2. When <u>are</u> you going to live in it?

3. _____

4. _____

5. _____

6. _____

7. _____

8. _____

Now write two sentences using <u>it's</u> and its. <u>Remember</u>: <u>It's</u> is a contraction of <u>it is,</u> and <u>its</u> is a possessive pronoun.

1. _____

2. _____

3. _____

4. _____

© Summer Bridge Activities™ 4-5   27   www.summerbrains.com

Day 13

A Trip to Outer Space. We're planning a big trip into outer space! You are invited to come along, too. You can even invite a few friends. What will you pack? Why? Where shall we go? What needs to be done? What do you think will happen? What will it be like? Think, then write!

Problem solving.

1. Jennifer bought a package of candy for $2.50. The tax was 19¢. She used a coupon for 42¢ off the price of the candy. How much did she pay? _____

2. Elsie worked at a grocery store keeping the shelves full. She worked 4 hours on Wednesday and 5 hours on Friday. She earned $5 an hour. How much did she earn that week? _____

3. Randy bought a box of cookies for $1.98. He used a 20¢ coupon on "Double Coupon Day." On this particular day, the store took off double the coupon's value. How much did Randy pay for that box of cookies? _____

4. Bradley bought a shirt for $5 off the original price of $24. The tax was $1.40. How much did Bradley pay? _____

5. Gayle bought a 6 pack of canned orange juice for $2.89. The store had a special for 74¢ off the original price. The tax was 60¢. How much did Gayle spend? _____

Match the word to the meaning. Use a dictionary.

EXAMPLE:

1. honorable
2. current
3. knowledge
4. suspicion
5. exact
6. lantern
7. profession
8. universal
9. agriculture
10. declare
11. wilderness
12. ordinary
13. comical
14. tremendous
15. generation

a kind of light
occupation, source of livelihood
to make clearly known
good reputation
usual, familiar, common
very large, great
leaving no room for error
now in progress
uninhabited region
all the people born about the same time
information, awareness, understanding
humorous, funny
understood by all
the science and art of farming
suspecting or being suspected

Here are some words you should know how to spell. Read the meanings below and see if you know what the words mean. Write the word by its meaning.

gnaw	doubt	knit	gnat	glisten	plain
pause	pedal	scene	tow	comfort	admire

1. make something with long needles out of yarn _____
2. to have high regard for with wonder and delight _____
3. a lever worked with the foot _____
4. shine or sparkle _____
5. to not believe; to feel unsure _____
6. a short stop or wait _____
7. to pull by a rope or chain _____
8. freedom from hardship; to ease _____
9. flatland; not fancy _____
10. part of a play; show strong feelings in front of others _____
11. to bite at something or wear away _____
12. small fly or insect _____

Continents. **Have you ever really looked at the shapes of the continents on a world map? It almost seems as if the continents are part of a big puzzle. Find a world map, then trace and cut out the following major continents and islands: North and South America, Australia, Europe-Asia, Greenland, and Africa. Try to fit all of the continents together so that no (or very little) space exists between them.**

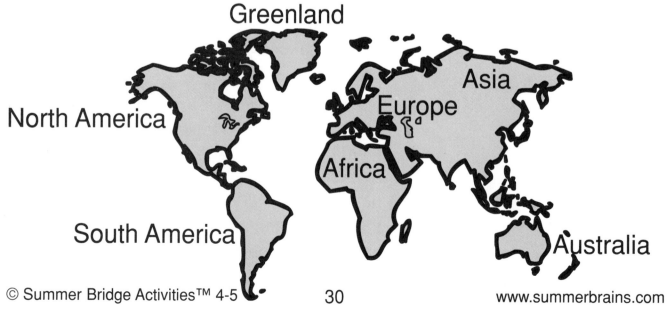

Divide to find the quotient.

1. 4)28   2. 5)40   3. 7)49   4. 6)30

5. 8)72   6. 9)45   7. 8)32   8. 3)15

9. 7)56   10. 6)24   11. 7)14   12. 6)54

13. 9)9   14. 7)28   15. 6)42   16. 8)56

17. 7)35   18. 6)48   19. 9)81   20. 8)24

21. 8)40   22. 9)72   23. 7)63   24. 7)42

You have been out of school for a few weeks now. Write a story telling what you have been doing for the past few weeks. Be sure to follow the five steps of the writing process.

_____

_____

_____

_____

_____

_____

_____

_____

_____

_____

Below are the days of the week and the months of the year spelled from dictionary symbols. Write the words to the side. Don't forget capital letters. The first one is done for you.

1. /ā´prəl/ _____*April*_____   11. /märch/ _____

2. /jan´ūre´ē/ _____   12. /wenz´dā/ _____

3. /mun´dā/ _____   13. /jün/ _____

4. /sep tem´bər/ _____   14. /sun´dā/ _____

5. /dē sem´bər/ _____   15. /nō vem´bər/ _____

6. /sat´ər dā/ _____   16. /o´gest/ _____

7. /mā/ _____   17. /thərz´dā/ _____

8. /feb´rüer´ē/ _____   18. /ok tō bər/ _____

9. /tūz´dā/ _____   19. /jülī´/ _____

10. /frī´dā/ _____

Rocks. **Rocks are found almost everywhere. There is much to see and learn about rocks. Geologists are scientists who study rocks. All rocks are made up of one or more minerals. Scientists have discovered over 2,000 minerals. Rocks are changed by water, plants, and other forces of nature. Below are words you need to know when talking about rocks. Look up each word in the dictionary and write down a short definition of it.**

1. igneous _____

2. sedimentary _____

3. metamorphic _____

4. mineral _____

5. crystal _____

6. lava _____

7. magma _____

8. anthracite _____

9. bituminous _____

10. coal _____

Words to Sound, Read, and Spell

ability	comedian	erosion	gravel
accent	commentator	esophagus	graze
acre	convince	essay	gulf
active	cough	estimate	hailstone
adobe	cultural	evaporate	hare
agent	curator	exquisite	harmony
aluminum	custodian	facial	harpsichord
amendment	customs	factor	heirloom
ancestor	dazzling	fake	hemisphere
anchor	deafening	fantasy	herb
appearance	decision	fare	homesteader
appliance	defend	faucet	illustrator
artery	delegate	festival	immigration
assemble	denominator	fever	immune
assuage	deposit	fiction	importance
atmosphere	depth	folklore	income
awkward	desperate	forlorn	incorrect
ballad	diameter	fragile	industry
ballot	diary	freighter	inheritance
barracuda	digit	fret	intersect
bashful	disapprove	frontier	juggler
blunder	disaster	frown	jute
brave	disgraceful	galleon	laboratory
bronze	display	garlic	laryngitis
cafeteria	dormitory	germ	legend
calculator	dose	getaway	lengthen
camouflage	downhearted	ginger	liberty
candidate	drowsy	glamorous	license
canvas	dungeon	gland	lightning
carpenter	earnings	global	limestone
cartoonist	election	grammar	linen
chemical	elegant	grandstand	livestock
clue	engineer	granite	lotion

Words to Sound, Read, and Spell

lounge	parakeet	salve	tarantula
luscious	parallel	sameness	telecast
mainland	parentheses	scale	tender
marble	password	schwa	theft
marionette	percale	scrapbook	thrush
mathematics	percussion	scrawny	title
meadowlark	perimeter	sculptor	torrent
megaphone	permission	seaway	tortilla
membrane	pharmacist	section	tract
memoir	pianist	self-confidence	translator
messenger	population	shipbuilding	transplant
meteor	prescription	shiver	transport
metric	press	shortage	treasurer
migration	pretend	signature	tributary
minerals	professor	slender	tricot
misplace	pronounce	smear	uncertain
mosquito	prop	sodden	uncomfortable
musician	puppet	soggy	unexpected
muslin	quotation	solution	unimportant
mystery	quotient	solve	uninvited
narrator	radius	spatula	unkind
nonsense	rattan	spice	utensils
numerator	recipe	spine	verse
nurse	recount	statehood	vertex
nursery	regional	statue	vessel
nylon	representative	stupid	visible
obedience	reservoir	suffer	vitamin
ointment	revenge	sunbeam	vowel
orchard	roam	supermarket	voyage
organ	rodent	surround	wept
outline	rotation	talent	wickedness
oxen	rumble	tambourine	woodwind
painter	saddle	tangerine	yogurt

Summer Bridge Activities™
Incentive Contract Calendar

Month _____

My parents and I decided that if I complete 20 days of
Summer Bridge Activities™ and read _____ minutes a day,
my incentive/reward will be:

_____

Child's Signature _____
Parent's Signature _____

Day 1	📖	⭐	——	Day 11	📖	⭐	——
Day 2	📖	⭐	——	Day 12	📖	⭐	——
Day 3	📖	⭐	——	Day 13	📖	⭐	——
Day 4	📖	⭐	——	Day 14	📖	⭐	——
Day 5	📖	⭐	——	Day 15	📖	⭐	——
Day 6	📖	⭐	——	Day 16	📖	⭐	——
Day 7	📖	⭐	——	Day 17	📖	⭐	——
Day 8	📖	⭐	——	Day 18	📖	⭐	——
Day 9	📖	⭐	——	Day 19	📖	⭐	——
Day 10	📖	⭐	——	Day 20	📖	⭐	——

Child: Color the ⭐ for daily activities completed.
Color the 📖 for daily reading completed.

Parent: Initial the _____ for daily activities and reading
your child completes.

1. Get a piece of paper that is as long and as wide as you. Lie down on it and have someone outline you with a marker. Then color in the details--eyes, ears, mouth, clothes, arms, hands, etc.

2. Make a "Happy Birthday" card for a friend who is celebrating a birthday, and give it to that person on his or her special day.

3. Invite your friends over for popcorn and vote on your favorite Disney movie. Watch the winning movie, then choose parts and act out the movie in your own way.

4. Visit the library and attend story time.

5. With bright colored markers, draw a picture of your favorite place to go. Paste it to a piece of posterboard and cut it into pieces for a jigsaw puzzle.

Fun Activity Ideas to Go Along with the Second Section!

6. Give your dog a bath or ask your neighbor or friend if you can give their dog a bath.

7. Pack a lunch and go to the park.

8. Roast marshmallows over a fire or barbecue.

9. Draw the shape of your state and put a star where you live. Draw your state flower, motto, and bird.

10. Make a batch of cookies and take them to a sick friend, neighbor, or relative.

11. Plant some flower or vegetable seeds in a pot and watch them grow.

12. Organize an earthquake drill for your family.

13. Pick one of your favorite foods and learn how to make it.

14. Write a poem that rhymes.

15. Get your neighborhood friends together and make a card of appreciation for the firestation closest to you. Then all of you deliver the card and take a tour of the station.

16. Prepare a clean bed for your pet.

17. Make and fly a kite.

18. Read to younger children in your family or neighborhood.

19. Invent a new game and play it with your friends.

20. Surprise a family member with breakfast in bed.

Write the rest of the number families. The first one is done for you.

1. 6 x 9 = 54	2. 7 x 8 = 56	3. 6 x 7 = 42	4. 63 ÷ 9 = 7
9 x 6 = 54	_____	_____	_____
54 ÷ 6 = 9	_____	_____	_____
54 ÷ 9 = 6	_____	_____	_____
5. 48 ÷ 6 = 8	6. 72 ÷ 8 = 9	7. 6 x 9 = 54	8. 32 ÷ 8 = 4
_____	_____	_____	_____
_____	_____	_____	_____
_____	_____	_____	_____
9. 36 ÷ 4 = 9	9. 9 x 7 = 63	11. 5 x 9 = 45	12. 90 ÷ 9 = 10
_____	_____	_____	_____
_____	_____	_____	_____
_____	_____	_____	_____

Prefixes and suffixes. <u>Remember</u>: Prefixes are added to the beginning of a base word. Suffixes are added to the end of a base word. Add a prefix to these words. Use: mis-, un-, and re-. Write the whole word.

1. lucky _____
2. spell _____
3. build _____

4. judge _____
5. fill _____
6. able _____

Add a suffix to these words. Use: -er, -less, -ful, and -ed. Write the whole word.

7. use _____
8. care _____
9. sing _____
10. spell _____

11. hope _____
12. teach _____
13. paint _____
14. report _____

Now write two sentences using words of your choice from each of the two word lists above.

1. _____
2. _____

Opinions. **Everyone has an opinion on most things that happen around them. People will listen to your opinion more often if you state clearly and plainly why you feel as you do.**

Write your opinion on one of the following topics or choose one of your own to write about.

1. People should always wear seatbelts.
2. Children should be able to eat anything they want.
3. Schoolchildren should never have homework to do.
4. We should always help other people whether they are in our country or not.

_____

_____

_____

_____

_____

_____

_____

_____

_____

_____

_____

_____

_____

_____

_____

_____

_____

_____

_____

_____

_____

_____

Find the product by multiplying.

EXAMPLE:					
1 12 x 6 72	1. 12 x 4	2. 22 x 6	3. 18 x 2	4. 23 x 4	5. 42 x 5

6. 23
x 7

7. 34
x 6

8. 16
x 5

9. 78
x 5

10. 93
x 6

11. 86
x 7

12. 69
x 9

13. 57
x 4

14. 62
x 6

15. 97
x 7

16. 75
x 8

17. 33
x 3

18. 21
x 5

19. 85
x 8

20. 68
x 9

21. 45
x 3

22. 99
x 9

Think of your five senses to describe the words below. Try to come up with a word for each sense.

EXAMPLE:	taste	touch	smell	sight	sound
Fire	smoky	hot	smoky	bright	crackle
Candy Bar	sweet	smooth	chocolate	brown	crunchy

1. a red rose _____

2. a rainbow _____

3. a barnyard_____

4. a snake's skin _____

5. rollerblades _____

6. a snowflake _____

Choose one of the above and write a paragraph about it. Be very descriptive and put in a lot of details.

_____

_____

_____

_____

Prefixes and suffixes can be added to word parts as well as base or root words. Add a prefix or suffix to these word parts, then find and fill in the word shapes below.

1. *du* plex
2. __ __ mit
3. don __ __
4. sel __ __ __

5. pott __ __ __
6. __ __ __ gress
7. __ __ __ tant
8. syll __ __ __ __

9. __ __ __ dora
10. gran __ __ __
11. __ __ plicate
12. __ __ sent

13. __ __ most
14. fur __ __ __ __
15. __ __ do
16. sta __ __ __ __

d u p l e x

Mystery Word. Read the following clues to discover the mystery word.

1. The top layer of the earth's surface.
2. It's composed of mineral particles mixed with animal and plant matter.
3. A well-organized, complicated layer of debris covering most of the earth's land surface.
4. It is shallow in some places and deep in other places.
5. It can be very red or very black, as well as other shades and colors.
6. It is one of the most important natural resources of any country.
7. It is so important that we need to make great efforts to conserve it.
8. It takes a long time for it to form.
9. There are different kinds or types.
10. A geologist thinks of it as materials that cover the solid rock below the earth's surface.
11. The engineer thinks of it as materials on which to build buildings, roads, earth dams, and landing strips.
12. To the farmer and most other people, it is a thin layer of the earth's surface that supports the growth of all kinds of plants.

The Mystery Word is:

Complete the tables.

1. There are 5 pennies in a nickel.

pennies	5	10	15	20	25	30
nickels	1					

2. There are 10 dimes in a dollar.

dimes	10	20	30			
dollars	1	2				

3. There are 6 cans of pop in each carton.

cans	6	12		24		36
cartons	1		3		5	

4. You can get 6 swimming lessons for $20.

lessons	6	12	18			36
money	$20			$80	$100	

When you write something, your reader should be able to understand clearly what you are trying to say. Read the sentences below and change the underlined word to a more descriptive or exact word.

EXAMPLE: This is a good book.
This is an awesome book.

1. My teacher is nice. _____

2. Your things will be safe here. _____

3. That is a big building. _____

4. A car went by our house. _____

5. Our pictures of the trip turned out bad. _____

6. This is a good sandwich. _____

7. The little boy saw a pretty butterfly. _____

8. Many big worms were crawling on the ground. _____

9. We had a bad winter. _____

10. These grapes are awful. _____

Day 3

Most words spelled backwards don't mean anything, but some do. Here are clues for some words that become different words when they are written backwards. The first one is done for you.

1. Spell a word backwards for something you cook in and you will have a word that means siesta. _pan_ & _nap_

2. Spell a word backwards for a name and you will have something you turn on to get water. _____ & _____

3. Spell a word backwards for something you catch a fish in and you will have a number. _____ & _____

4. Spell a word backwards for something to carry things in and you will get a word that tells what you like to do with your friends. _____ & _____

5. Spell a word backwards for something a train needs and you will get a word for someone who is not honest. _____ & _____

6. Spell a word backwards for victory and you will have a word that means "at once." _____ & _____

7. Spell a word backwards for something to catch a mouse in and you will get a word that means something less than whole. _____ & _____

8. Spell a word backwards for a tool that cuts wood and you will get a word that is a verb. _____ & _____

9. Spell a word backwards for a flying mammal and you will get a word that means "a bill or check." _____ & _____

10. Spell a word backwards for the end of your pen and you will have a word that means a hole in the ground. _____ & _____

11. Spell a word backwards that means something you bathe in and you will have a word that means "other than." _____ & _____

12. Spell a word backwards for "an instrument used in doing work" and you will get a word that means "things taken in a robbery." _____ & _____

13. Spell a word backwards for something that means "to have life" and you will get a word that means wicked. _____ & _____

14. Spell a word backwards for a word that means "a girl" and you will have a word that means to "fall behind." _____ & _____

Measuring in centimeters. Your little finger is about 1 centimeter wide. If you don't have a centimeter tape, use a string and this centimeter ruler to measure the following activities.

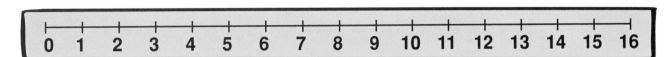

1. The length of your shoes _____
2. The length and width of this book _____, _____
3. Your neck measurement _____
4. Your waist measurement _____
5. Your kitchen table length and width _____, _____
6. The width of a chair in your home _____
7. Your height in centimeters _____
8. The length of the pencil or pen that you use _____

How many other things can you measure? Try estimating, then check to see how close you come to the exact measurement.

_____
_____
_____
_____

Underline the pronouns in the following sentences. <u>Remember</u>: **A pronoun takes the place of a noun.**

1. Will you go with us?
2. He did a good job.
3. She went with me.
4. We ate all of them.
5. It is time for her to go.
6. They will help us today.
7. I thanked him for it.
8. You and I need to hurry.
9. Tomorrow we will go home.
10. This book came for him.
11. A package came for us.
12. You are a good sport.
13. He and I ate the apples.
14. Animals like them also.
15. It was very good.
16. How did she do?

The Fourth of July is our nation's birthday. Another name for it is spelled out in the boxes of the puzzle. Finish the puzzle by writing the appropriate words from the word box. You will not use all of the words.

death
breath
nickel
field
either
startle
worth
sandal
medal
stroke
sprinkle
tongue
clumsy
ankle
partner
shuffle
whether
guard
mumble
burglar
quarter
plural
prompt
rather
greedy
daughter
scramble
couple

I
N
D
E
P
E
N
D
E
N
C
E
D
A
Y

Bugs, Bugs, and More Bugs. The world has so many different kinds of bugs, but there's always room for one more. Create a brand new type of bug. Describe it. Where does it live? What does it do? What does it eat? How does it survive? Who are its friends or enemies?

Multiplying with tens and hundreds is fast and fun.

1. 4 x 10 = _____
2. 600 x 6 = _____
3. 7 x 800 = _____
4. 30 x 8 = _____
5. 5 x 20 = _____
6. 800 x 5 = _____
7. 8 x 90 = _____
8. 50 x 6 = _____
9. 600 x 5 = _____
10. 4 x 100 = _____
11. 7 x 80 = _____
12. 7 x 500 = _____
13. 900 x 7 = _____
14. 600 x 4 = _____
15. 900 x 4 = _____
16. 8 x 900 = _____
17. 800 x 2 = _____
18. 7 x 900 = _____
19. 3 x 10 = _____
20. 700 x 6 = _____
21. 3 x 800 = _____
22. 7 x 40 = _____
23. 9 x 10 = _____
24. 10 x 100 = _____
25. 4 x 60 = _____
26. 80 x 2 = _____
27. 500 x 4 = _____
28. 7 x 700 = _____
29. 30 x 8 = _____
30. 800 x 6 = _____
31. 9 x 500 = _____
30. 9 x 300 = _____
33. 300 x 5 = _____

Pronouns, such as I, you, he, she, it, we, and they, can be the subject of a sentence. Read these sentences. The subject is underlined. Rewrite the sentences and use a subject pronoun in place of the underlined subject. Write in cursive.

1. Jim and I went fishing with our dad.

_____

2. The weather was sunny and warm.

_____

3. Ann and Sue can help us with the bait.

_____

4. Mr. Jack broke his leg.

_____

5. Kathy is going to New York on a vacation.

_____

6. Ryan will paint the scenery.

_____

Categorize these words under one of the headings. Hint: There can be eight words under each heading. Remember: Categorizing words means to put them in groups that have something in common. One row of examples is given.

interstate	add	region	colony	oxygen	solid
bacteria	city	hemisphere	stop	column	inch
debate	larva	yield	basin	hexagon	canal
environment	speed	equal	fossil	candidate	intersection
measure	insect	bay	caution	map	estimate
numerator	freedom	society	elevation	freeway	railroad
patriot	habitat	civilization	mineral	detour	quotient

Math Words	Geography Words	Transportation Words	Science Words	Social Studies Words
add	*region*	*interstate*	*bacteria*	*colony*

What About These Animals in Our Country. **Buffalo, condors, and grizzly bears have all but disappeared from our country. The symbol of our country, the bald eagle, is very rare in most states. Bald eagles and bears live in mountainous regions. Prairie dogs and antelope live in the plain regions. Alligators live in marshy areas. Rattlesnakes live in the desert. Wild turkeys can be found in wilderness areas. These are all animals found in our country. There are also many others. Choose one of the following to do on a separate piece of paper.**

1. Choose and draw a picture of an animal from our country. Place it in the correct habitat. Color it accurately. What other interesting animals do you think might belong in this area? Draw them. What other important information does your picture show?

2. If you choose not to draw a picture about an animal, write a paragraph about one. Use the same type of information that the picture would portray.

What animal(s) did you choose? _____

_____

Addition and multiplication are related. Answer the addition problems and then write the related multiplication problem.

EXAMPLE: 10 + 10 + 10 + 10 + 10 = 50; 5 x 10 = 50

1. 20 + 20 + 20 = _____   _____ x _____ = _____

2. 9 + 9 + 9 + 9 + 9 + 9 = _____   _____ x _____ = _____

3. 100 + 100 + 100 + 100 = _____   _____ x _____ = _____

4. 8 + 8 + 8 + 8 + 8 + 8 + 8 + 8 = _____   _____ x _____ = _____

5. 12 + 12 + 12 + 12 = _____   _____ x _____ = _____

6. 75 + 75 + 75 = _____   _____ x _____ = _____

7. 35 + 35 + 35 + 35 + 35 + 35 = _____   _____ x _____ = _____

8. 51 + 51 + 51 + 51 + 51 = _____   _____ x _____ = _____

Use pronouns me, her, him, it, us, you, and them after action verbs. Use I and me after the other nouns or pronouns. Circle the correct pronoun in each sentence.

1. Lily and (I, me) like to visit museums.
2. (They, Them) were very juicy oranges.
3. He helped her and (I, me).
4. (We, Us) tried not to fall as much this time.
5. Miss Green gave a shovel and bucket to (he, him).
6. (I, Me) wanted a new horse for Christmas.
7. Rick asked (she, her) to come with us.
8. Jason went with (they, them) to the mountain.
9. Mother asked (I, me) to fix the dinner.
10. Carla got some forks for (we, us).
11. Please, teach that trick to Lisa and (I, me).
12. She and (I, me) swam all day.

me   her

him   it

us

you

them

Study this table about trees, and use it to answer the questions below. Can you identify the trees around you?

Tree	Bark	Wood	Leaves
Elm	brown and rough	strong	oval-shaped, saw-toothed edges, sharp points
Birch	creamy white, peels off in layers	elastic, won't break easily	heart-shaped or triangular with pointed tips
Oak	dark gray, thick, rough, deeply furrowed	hard, fine-grained	round, finger-shaped lobes
Willow (Pussy Willow)	rough and broken	brown, soft, light	long, narrow, curved at tips
Maple	rough gray	strong	grow in pairs and are shaped like your open hand
Hickory	loose, peels off	white, hard	shaped like spearheads
Christmas Holly	ash colored	hard and fine-grained	glossy, sharp-pointed

1. Which tree has heart-shaped leaves? _____ Hand-shaped?

   _____

2. How many trees have hard wood? _____

3. Which trees have sharp-pointed leaves? _____

4. Which tree has wood like a rubber band? _____

5. How many different colors of bark does the table show? _____

   Name them _____

6. Which tree do you think we get syrup from? _____

7. Which tree bark do you think Indians used to cover their canoes?

   _____

8. Which wood do you think is best for making furniture? _____,

   _____, and _____

9. Why do you think the holly tree is called Christmas Holly? _____

10. Look around your yard and neighborhood. Can you identify any of the trees

    from the above table? If so, which ones? _____

Complete this multiplication table.

x	10	20	30	40	50	60	70	80	90
1	10	20					70		
2						120			
3		60							270
4				160					
5							350		
6									
7			210						
8						480			
9				360					

How does multiplying by hundreds differ from multiplying by tens?

_____

Could you change this table to show multiplying by hundreds? _____

How? _____

Using Its, It's, Your, and You're. It's and you're are contractions. <u>Its</u> and <u>your</u> are possessive pronouns. **Fill in the blanks with <u>it's</u>, <u>its</u>, <u>your</u>, or <u>you're</u>**

1. I hope _____ coming to my barn dance.

2. The dance will be for _____ friends also.

3. Do you think _____ too cold for a barn dance?

4. _____ starting time is eight o'clock.

5. Will _____ family come to the dance with you?

6. _____ floor is long and wide.

7. _____ coming early, aren't you?

8. I think I will need _____ help.

9. _____ going to last about four hours.

10. _____ bound to be a lot of fun.

Write a sentence of your own for each word.

11. it's_____

12. its _____

13. you're _____

14. your _____

Read this crazy story. Every time you come to an underlined word, write the abbreviation for it. The first one is done for you.

Last January _Jan._ we moved from Georgia _____ to New York _____. It was a very long trip. We had to walk most of the way because the car broke down. We left on Monday _____, March _____ 10 and didn't get there until five years _____ later.

On the trip I had to learn how to measure. One day I measured gallons _____, inches, _____, yards _____, and grams _____. I also learned about science _____, adverbs _____, and adjectives _____. It was a boring trip!

We only traveled about two miles per hour _____. That's why it took us so long. Also, we stopped at a number _____ of relatives' places and stayed for months _____ on end.

Next time let's fly!

● ●

Name an animal or insect that begins with the letters given. If there is not one that begins with that letter, leave it blank or put an *X* in the box.

	s	d	r	t
insects				
birds				
reptiles				
rodents				
spiders				
zoo animals				
wild animals				
farm animals				
ocean animals				
dinosaurs				

What About Time? You know that 60 seconds = 1 minute, 60 minutes = 1 hour, 24 hours = 1 day, 7 days = 1 week, 52 weeks = 1 year, 12 months = 1 year, and 365 days = 1 year (except leap year, which has 366 days).

Day 8

Use what you know to complete the following.

1. Phillip is in the fourth grade. He is 10 _____ old.
2. There are 30 _____ in June.
3. Nancy's baby brother started to walk at the age of 11 _____.
4. We have 48 _____ in two days.
5. Nick's swimming lesson is 25 _____ long.
6. It took Leslie 10 _____ to comb her hair.
7. Mother's Day is celebrated once a _____.
8. Many children get about 3 _____ summer vacation.
9. It takes about 1 _____ to blink your eyes.
10. Most children go to school 5 _____ a week.
11. There are 30 _____ in half a minute.
12. It took Monica 2 and a half _____ to do all her chores.

Write these words in alphabetical order. Be sure to look at the third or fourth letters.

1. events, evening, every, eventually

   _____ _____ _____ _____

2. tremendous, treatment, tree, treasure

   _____ _____ _____ _____

3. coast, coconut, coal, collect, color

   _____ _____ _____ _____ _____

4. entrance, entry, end, enthusiasm, enough

   _____ _____ _____ _____ _____

5. grandfather, graph, grain, grateful, grab, graduated

   _____ _____ _____ _____ _____ _____

What Does It Really Mean?
Write what you think these idiomatic expressions mean.

1. She was really <u>pulling</u> <u>my</u> <u>leg</u>. _____

2. Do you think we'll <u>be</u> <u>in</u> <u>hot</u> <u>water</u>? _____

3. If you don't <u>button</u> <u>your</u> <u>lip</u>, I'll scream! _____

4. Sonny, please <u>get</u> <u>off</u> <u>my</u> <u>back</u>! _____

5. When you are having fun, <u>time</u> <u>flies</u>. _____

6. You've <u>hit</u> <u>it</u> <u>on</u> <u>the</u> <u>head</u>, Andrew. _____

7. Ryan will <u>lend</u> <u>a</u> <u>hand</u> tomorrow. _____

8. In the winter, my bedroom is <u>like</u> <u>an</u> <u>icebox</u>. _____

9. Mrs. Tune always has beautiful flowers; she <u>must</u> <u>have</u> <u>a</u> <u>green</u> <u>thumb</u>.

_____

10. My brother's stomach is <u>a</u> <u>bottomless</u> <u>pit</u>. _____

✦ ✦

A Litter Graph.
Go on a "litter" walk. In a plastic bag, gather up litter as you go. Only pick up <u>safe</u> litter. Do not pick up anything marked hazardous waste, needles or litter you are unsure of. When you are finished, bring it home. Categorize what you have found and display it in a bar graph.

Name of Litter	1	2	3	4	5	6	7	8	9	10	more than 10

Place value division patterns. We know that 8 ÷ 2 = 4 so 80 ÷ 2 = 40 and 800 ÷ 2 = 400. Do the following division patterns.

1. 9 ÷ 3 = _____   90 ÷ 3 = _____   900 ÷ 3 = _____
2. 8 ÷ 2 = _____   80 ÷ 2 = _____   800 ÷ 2 = _____
3. 12 ÷ 4 = _____   120 ÷ 4 = _____   1200 ÷ 4 = _____
4. 6 ÷ 3 = _____   60 ÷ 3 = _____   600 ÷ 3 = _____
5. 30 ÷ 6 = _____   300 ÷ 6 = _____   3000 ÷ 6 = _____
6. 72 ÷ 8 = _____   720 ÷ 8 = _____   7200 ÷ 8 = _____
7. 32 ÷ 8 = _____   320 ÷ 8 = _____   3200 ÷ 8 = _____
8. 49 ÷ 7 = _____   490 ÷ 7 = _____   4900 ÷ 7 = _____
9. 56 ÷ 8 = _____   560 ÷ 8 = _____   5600 ÷ 8 = _____
10. 25 ÷ 5 = _____   250 ÷ 5 = _____   2500 ÷ 5 = _____
11. 40 ÷ 8 = _____   400 ÷ 8 = _____   4000 ÷ 8 = _____
12. 63 ÷ 9 = _____   630 ÷ 9 = _____   6300 ÷ 9 = _____

Look up the word <u>meet</u> in a dictionary. It is at the end of each sentence, write the part of speech (noun or verb). Then write the number for the meaning of the word <u>meet</u>. The first one is done for you.

EXAMPLE: I will <u>meet</u> you at three.   *Verb – 2*

1. Tomorrow we are going to have a track <u>meet</u>.   _____
2. I hope he doesn't <u>meet</u> with disaster.   _____
3. We need to <u>meet</u> the plane at seven P.M.   _____
4. Did you go to the <u>meet</u> for the city council members?   _____
5. He will have to <u>meet</u> the payments every month.   _____
6. It was nice to <u>meet</u> and talk with you yesterday.   _____
7. Are you going to <u>meet</u> your friends later?   _____

Someone or Something With Power. **What is power? Choose something or someone with power. How do they have power? How did they get it? Could they lose it? Do they use it? How? Why? Do you have power? Yes you do! What are some of the powers that you have? What are some that you don't have that you would like to have?**

_____

_____

_____

_____

_____

_____

_____

_____

_____

_____

_____

_____

_____

_____

_____

_____

_____

_____

_____

_____

_____

_____

Find the quotients and the remainders of the quotients. Use a separate piece of paper to show your work.

EXAMPLE:

```
        12 R 2
    3 ) 38
        3
        8
        6
        2
```

3. 3) 95

8. 5) 58

4. 4) 85

9. 7) 79

5. 9) 100

10. 4) 87

1. 2) 65

6. 3) 37

11. 3) 68

2. 5) 57

7. 4) 47

12. 4) 35

Draw a line between the syllables. Try to <u>remember</u> what you have learned about where to divide them. Use a dictionary if you need help.

EXAMPLE: col/or

1. column	10. alphabet	19. generation
2. inflate	11. soviet	20. vegetable
3. slashing	12. bicycle	21. evidence
4. pigeon	13. difficult	22. memory
5. afraid	14. kerosene	23. quality
6. frozen	15. liveliness	24. splendid
7. tennis	16. glorious	25. museum
8. harness	17. understood	26. hospital
9. gable	18. jewelry	27. ordinary

The next time you watch T.V. or read a magazine, look at the commercials or ads. In the boxes below, write down what you think is true about the commercials or ads and what you think is false.

What is the commercial or ad about?	TRUE	FALSE
	1.	1.
	2.	2.
	3.	3.
	4.	4.
	5.	5.

Conserving Energy. Recycling saves energy and natural resources. Besides recycling, how can we conserve energy? Write down ways to conserve energy with the following resources.

water _____

lights _____

heat _____

electricity _____

transportation _____

cold weather _____

refrigerator _____

buying things _____

bathroom _____

Write the fraction that tells about the shaded section.

EXAMPLE:

1. $\frac{1}{2}$

2. _____

3. _____

4. _____

5. _____

6. _____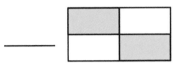

7. _____

8. _____

9. _____

10. _____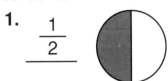

11. _____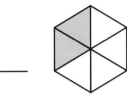

12. _____

A dictionary gives us a lot of information about words. Look up the following words in a dictionary and write down the special spelling of each. The words show you how many syllables. Also write down a short definition for each word.

	Special Spelling	Definition
1. blue•bon•net	**bloo′bon′net**	the cornflower
2. mas•sive	_____	_____
3. suit•case	_____	_____
4. cir•cus	_____	_____
5. glox•in•i•a	_____	_____
6. rig•ging	_____	_____
7. di•lem•ma	_____	_____
8. meas•ure	_____	_____
9. stu•dent	_____	_____
10. un•or•gan•ized	_____	_____
11. def•i•ni•tion	_____	_____
12. yaws	_____	_____
13. re•spect	_____	_____
14. blun•der•buss	_____	_____

Practice writing and spelling these homonyms. Write in cursive. After you know how to spell them, have someone give you a test to see if you can spell them without looking. Write each word twice.

way	_____ _____	sight	_____ _____
weigh	_____ _____	site	_____ _____
base	_____ _____	arc	_____ _____
bass	_____ _____	ark	_____ _____
threw	_____ _____	tide	_____ _____
through	_____ _____	tied	_____ _____
scene	_____ _____	waist	_____ _____
seen	_____ _____	waste	_____ _____
		sore	_____ _____
		soar	_____ _____
		pare	_____ _____
		pair	_____ _____
		pear	_____ _____

YOUR Test Score

Water in the Air. There is water in the air. How does it get there? Clouds and rain are made from water vapor in the air.

Try this to help explain how water gets into the air. Take 3 or more drinking glasses that are all about the same size. Fill the glasses almost full of water. Place them in different areas such as warm places, cool places, dark places, windy places, outside places, inside places, and other places of your choice. Watch them for 4 or 5 days or longer. Check the water levels. What happened to the water in the glasses? Where did it go? Explain in your own words where you think the water vapor in the atmosphere comes from and where it goes?

_____

_____

_____

_____

_____

_____

kitchen garden

Comparing fractions. **Use the fraction table to help find out which fraction is greater and which fraction is less. Use >, <, or =.**

1. $\dfrac{1}{2}$ ◯ $\dfrac{1}{4}$

2. $\dfrac{2}{3}$ ◯ $\dfrac{1}{3}$

3. $\dfrac{1}{4}$ ◯ $\dfrac{1}{6}$

4. $\dfrac{2}{6}$ ◯ $\dfrac{1}{3}$

5. $\dfrac{4}{8}$ ◯ $\dfrac{2}{10}$

6. $\dfrac{1}{12}$ ◯ $\dfrac{1}{10}$

7. $\dfrac{3}{4}$ ◯ $\dfrac{2}{8}$

8. $\dfrac{2}{5}$ ◯ $\dfrac{1}{3}$

9. $\dfrac{3}{8}$ ◯ $\dfrac{10}{12}$

10. $\dfrac{2}{8}$ ◯ $\dfrac{1}{4}$

11. $\dfrac{1}{5}$ ◯ $\dfrac{2}{10}$

12. $\dfrac{1}{3}$ ◯ $\dfrac{2}{4}$

13. $\dfrac{1}{6}$ ◯ $\dfrac{1}{3}$

14. $\dfrac{3}{12}$ ◯ $\dfrac{1}{3}$

15. $\dfrac{5}{10}$ ◯ $\dfrac{3}{6}$

16. $\dfrac{1}{2}$ ◯ $\dfrac{6}{10}$

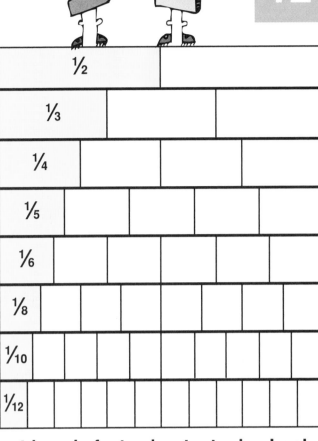

Write a short report. <u>**Remember**</u>**: A report is only facts about a topic. Look in an encyclopedia for help. Follow these steps: Choose a topic, plan, write, revise, proofread, and make a final copy.**

These letters are in alphabetical order. See if you can make a word from them. The first letter is underlined.

1. abbelo<u>pr</u> _____
2. ae<u>j</u>losu _____
3. eeenp<u>rr</u>st _____
4. beeemm<u>r</u>r _____
5. beknnor<u>u</u> _____
6. c<u>d</u>ffiilut _____
7. <u>a</u>ccdginor _____
8. ee<u>g</u>mnnort _____
9. aaegi<u>mn</u>z _____
10. eior<u>ss</u>u _____

11. ghho<u>tt</u>u _____
12. irst<u>w</u> _____
13. aeginr<u>v</u> _____
14. d<u>i</u>nrstuy _____
15. <u>c</u>eenrt _____
16. ehilst<u>w</u> _____
17. <u>a</u>inosux _____
18. deilor<u>s</u> _____
19. aa<u>b</u>eggg _____
20. elrtuu<u>v</u> _____

Put the letters in these words in alphabetical order.

21. creature _____
22. fountain _____
23. basement _____
24. factory _____

25. hospital _____
26. committee _____
27. paragraph _____
28. kingdom _____

Blow Up a Balloon. **Here is an experiment that you can do in your home with a parent's permission. Get a balloon and blow it up several times until the balloon becomes easy to enlarge. Put one tablespoon of baking soda in the balloon, then put 3 tablespoons of white vinegar into a soda pop bottle. Now put the balloon opening around the mouth of the soda pop bottle. Move the balloon so the baking soda falls down and mixes with the vinegar. Draw a picture of what happens and write a couple of sentences to go with your picture.**

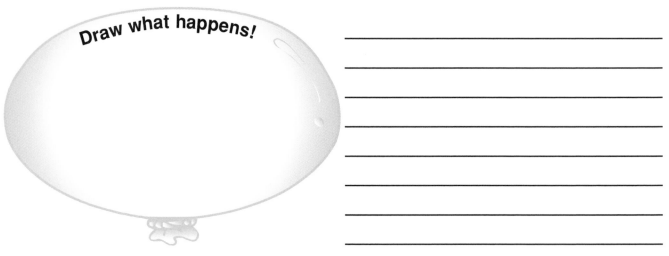

Draw what happens!

_____
_____
_____
_____
_____
_____
_____
_____

Multiplying 3 digit numbers by 1 digit numbers.

EXAMPLE: 6 x 3 = 18   3 x 80 = 240   3 x 100 = 300
18 + 240 + 300 = 558

1. 162
x 5

2. 398
x 2

3. 904
x 8

4. 329
x 5

5. 240
x 7

6. 432
x 6

7. 412
x 8

8. 542
x 9

9. 506
x 5

10. 554
x 6

11. 473
x 9

12. 257
x 8

Put commas in the following sentences to separate words in a series.

1. Nan Tom Julie and James are going to a movie.
2. Anne took her spelling reading and math books to school.
3. The snack bar is only open on Monday Tuesday Friday and Saturday.
4. Our new school flag is blue green yellow black and orange.
5. Women men children and pets enjoy sledding.
6. Have you ever seen baby kittens piglets or goslings?
7. Carla and Mark bought postcards film candy and souvenirs.

Now write four sentences of your own. Name at least three people, sports or foods in a series. Be sure to put in the commas.

8. _____
9. _____
10. _____
11. _____

Parents and Family. **What do you think your parents and family have in mind for your life? What do they want you to accomplish? What would they like to see you do? How do you feel about it? Think and write about it.**

How Many Times in a Minute? Use a watch with a minute hand or a stopwatch, to do the following activity. Then use the above information to calculate how many times you could do those things in 5 minutes, 8 minutes, 10 minutes and 15 minutes.

1. How far can you hop in a minute?

   _____

2. How far can you walk in a minute?

   _____

3. How many jumping jacks can you do in a minute?_____

4. How many times can you toss a ball and catch it in a minute?____

5. How many times can you bounce a ball in a minute? _____

6. How many times do you breathe in a minute? _____

7. How many times does your heart beat in a minute? _____

8. How many times can you write your name in a minute ? _____

Activity	Minutes				
	1	5	8	10	15
hop					
walk					
jumping jacks					
toss and catch ball					
bounce ball					
breathe					
heart beats					
write name					

Put commas after <u>yes</u> or <u>no</u> when they begin a sentence and after names when that person is being spoken to. Put the commas in these sentences.

1. Yes I will go with you John.
2. Kirk do you want to go?
3. No I need to finish this.
4. John I am glad Sam will come.
5. Nicky what happened?
6. Don I fell on the sidewalk.
7. Aaron do you play tennis?
8. No Eli I never learned how.
9. Come on B.J. let's go to the game.
10. Yes I was x-rayed at the doctor's.
11. Mom, thanks for the help.
12. Tell me Joe did you do this?
13. Yes but I'm sorry I did.
14. Well Joe try to be more careful next time.
15. Okay Dad I'll never do it again.
16. George do you like basketball?

Day 14

Do you know when the holidays come? Fill in the blanks with the date or name of the correct holiday. Use a calendar if you need help.

1. Many children look forward to _____ or _____ in December.

2. On January 1, we celebrate _____ _____ _____.

3. In May we have _____ _____.

4. Be sure to wear green in March. It's _____ _____ _____.

5. In October, 1492, he sailed the ocean blue. _____ _____.

6. On February 14, be sure to send your sweet heart a _____.

7. On July 4, we celebrate _____ _____.

8. October 31, can be really scary. _____.

9. Sometimes it comes in March; sometimes it comes in April: _____.

10. Do you work on _____ _____ in September?

11. _____ and _____ also have birthdays in February.

12. In June we also have _____ _____.

13. Martin Luther King Jr.'s birthday is in _____.

14. Because the Pilgrims came, we have _____.

15. _____ _____ is in June.

16. On November 11 we honor our _____.

Word Search. **Find and circle words that bring harm to our environment.**

c	a	r	s	i		p	o	c	a	l	o	c	t	w
j		l	o	p	p	o	s	f		i	d	h	s	r
f	a	c	t	o	r	i	e	s	g	t	a	d	n	a
p	k	n	s	l	a	s	w	a	s	t	e		s	p
l	c	g		l	g	o	a	e	b	e	i	e	h	p
r	a	q	s	u	u	n	g	d	w	r	l	m	l	e
b	r	n	b	t	m	k	e	s	i	t	t	e	a	r
b	a	t	j	i	l	l	k	m	t	b	k	m	n	s
c	a	r	b	o	n		m	o	n	o	x	i	d	e
v	u	a	f	n	j	c	b	g	m	e		s	f	a
p	t	s	f	l	o	o	d	s	i	d	l	g	i	z
s	o	h	s	t	r	i	n	g	r	a	g	s	l	r
t		s	p	e	o	p	l	e	c	s	t	y	l	t
u	e	t	r	p	e	s	t	i	c	i	d	e	s	s
g	x	v	e	c	k		m	a	n	c	f	o	e	n
n	h	x	o	n	a	e	h	g	l	a	s	s	e	o
o	a	c	u	b	h	g	a	r	b	a	g	e	u	t
w	u	j	a	c	f	a	c	t		p	a	p	e	r
	s	t	y	r	o	f	o	a	m	v	a	r	m	a
s	t	u	f	f		g	n	p	l	a	s	t	i	c

litter   gum
bottles   cartons
garbage   poison
trash   chemicals
cars   paper
people   styrofoam
rags   pesticides
smoke   sewage
waste   bags
pollution   smog
cans   weeds
landfills   floods
stuff   wrappers
junk   plastic
auto exhaust   string
carbon monoxide   glass
factories

Find the quotient and the remainder by division.

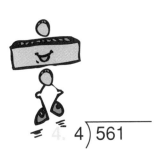

1. 8⟌963

2. 2⟌741

3. 8⟌960

4. 4⟌561

5. 7⟌915

6. 8⟌887

7. 5⟌753

8. 4⟌882

9. 9⟌918

10. 7⟌716

11. 3⟌919

12. 9⟌908

13. 4⟌835

14. 9⟌967

15. 8⟌842

16. 3⟌667

17. 5⟌182

18. 6⟌424

19. 4⟌392

20. 6⟌438

21. 7⟌948

22. 6⟌787

23. 4⟌721

24. 8⟌736

Using punctuation marks. Put periods and question, exclamation, and quotation marks in the following sentences.

1. Nate, do you have the map of our town asked Kit

2. What an exciting day I had cried Mary

3. I said the puppy fell into the well

4. Did you learn that birds' bones are hollow asked Mrs. Tippy

5. She answered No, I did not learn that

6. Wayne exclaimed I won first prize for the pie eating contest

7. I'm tired of all work and no play said Sadie

8. I agree with you replied Sarah

9. Mr. Harris said this assignment is due tomorrow

10. It will be part of your final grade he added

Circle the two words in each group that are spelled correctly.

A	B	C	D	E
gabel	suger	allready	where	jackit
genuine	surpize	among	weather	junior
gracefull	terrible	aunte	wite	jujment
graine	straight	awhile	weare	justece
great	sonday	addvise	rotee	journey

F	G	H	I	J
rimind	feathers	donkiys	handsum	explore
remain	feever	doubble	herrd	elctrecity
fouff	finsih	drawer	holiday	enjine
refer	folow	dosen	healthy	enormous
raisd	fiction	detective	haevy	ecstat

Complete the picture and add what other details you would like.

Equal Fractions. **Use the fraction table on page 59 to find equal fractions. You could make your own fraction table!**

1. $\dfrac{1}{3} = \dfrac{}{6}$ 2. $\dfrac{4}{5} = \dfrac{}{10}$ 3. $\dfrac{10}{10} = \dfrac{}{6}$ 4. $\dfrac{}{5} = \dfrac{4}{10}$

5. $\dfrac{4}{16} = \dfrac{}{8}$ 6. $\dfrac{12}{12} = \dfrac{}{10}$ 7. $\dfrac{3}{6} = \dfrac{}{12}$ 8. $\dfrac{9}{12} = \dfrac{}{4}$

9. $\dfrac{}{9} = \dfrac{4}{6}$ 10. $\dfrac{0}{4} = \dfrac{}{2}$ 11. $\dfrac{6}{8} = \dfrac{}{4}$ 12. $\dfrac{1}{2} = \dfrac{}{10}$

13. $\dfrac{}{4} = \dfrac{4}{8}$ 14. $\dfrac{3}{9} = \dfrac{}{3}$ 15. $\dfrac{}{15} = \dfrac{2}{3}$ 16. $\dfrac{2}{3} = \dfrac{}{12}$

17. $\dfrac{}{3} = \dfrac{6}{18}$ 18. $\dfrac{}{15} = \dfrac{3}{5}$ 19. $\dfrac{}{6} = \dfrac{2}{3}$ 20. $\dfrac{}{8} = \dfrac{1}{4}$

21. $\dfrac{3}{6} = \dfrac{}{2}$ 22. $\dfrac{1}{3} = \dfrac{}{9}$ 23. $\dfrac{6}{9} = \dfrac{}{3}$ 24. $\dfrac{}{6} = \dfrac{3}{18}$

What Does It Mean? **Choose a word from the word bank and write it next to the correct meaning.**

Word Bank

schedule
assistant
campaign
approximately
hollow
exchange
university
venture
artificial
publicity
harness
estate
reputation
genuine

1. not natural, not real _____
2. a timed plan for a project _____
3. a giving or taking of one thing for another _____
4. esteem in which a person is commonly held _____
5. a person who serves or helps _____
6. really being what it is said to be; true or real _____
7. a series of organized, planned actions_____
8. to make information commonly known _____
9. near in position _____
10. an educational institution of the highest level _____
11. having a cavity within it, not solid _____
12. something on which a risk is taken _____
13. one's property or possessions _____
14. connects an animal to a plow or vehicle _____

Look at the homonyms you spelled on page 58. Choose five pairs of these and write a sentence for each one.

EXAMPLE: way/weigh

I could not see him; we were <u>way</u> down the road.
How much do you <u>weigh</u>?

1. _____

_____

2. _____

_____

3. _____

_____

4. _____

_____

5. _____

_____

First-Aid Kit. **Every home should have a first-aid kit. This enables the family to have many types of bandages and medicines in one place, should they be needed.**

Make a list of things you think should be in a first-aid kit. When you are finished, check with your parents to see if you have all the basic things listed for a first-aid kit. If your family has one, ask your parents to go through it with you. Discuss the difference between a first-aid kit and an emergency kit.

Adding Fractions.

$\frac{2}{3} + \frac{1}{3} = \frac{3}{3}$ ← add the numerator
← use the same denominator

1. $\frac{1}{3} + \frac{1}{3} =$

2. $\frac{1}{2} + \frac{1}{2} =$

3. $\frac{6}{12} + \frac{5}{12} =$

4. $\frac{6}{12} + \frac{7}{12} =$

5. $\frac{5}{8} + \frac{2}{8} =$

6. $\frac{3}{10} + \frac{4}{10} =$

7. $\frac{1}{6} + \frac{2}{6} =$

8. $\frac{11}{12} + \frac{11}{12} =$

9. $\frac{7}{10} + \frac{1}{10} =$

10. $\frac{1}{8} + \frac{6}{8} =$

11. $\frac{4}{9} + \frac{4}{9} =$

12. $\frac{7}{10} + \frac{6}{10} =$

13. $\frac{1}{4} + \frac{2}{4} =$

14. $\frac{4}{10} + \frac{5}{10} =$

15. $\frac{3}{8} + \frac{3}{8} =$

16. $\frac{2}{8} + \frac{4}{8} =$

17. $\frac{3}{6} + \frac{1}{6} =$

18. $\frac{4}{12} + \frac{5}{12} =$

19. $\frac{2}{8} + \frac{7}{8} =$

20. $\frac{8}{12} + \frac{5}{12} =$

21. $\frac{3}{12} + \frac{8}{12} =$

22. $\frac{3}{10} + \frac{3}{10} =$

23. $\frac{5}{9} + \frac{5}{9} =$

24. $\frac{5}{8} + \frac{7}{8} =$

Circle the abbreviations and titles in these sentences. <u>Remember:</u>
Abbreviations are short forms of words and usually begin with capital letters and end with periods.

1. Dr. Cox is my family doctor.
2. Do you live on Rocksberry Rd.?
3. My teacher's name is Ms. Hansen.
4. On Mon. we are taking a trip to Salt Lake City, Ut.
5. Will Mr. Harris sell his company to your parents?
6. Rick's birthday and mine are both on Feb. 16.

Now write the abbreviations for these words.

7. street _____

8. avenue _____

9. postscript _____

10. Miss _____

11. January _____

12. Thursday _____

13. Utah _____

14. Tuesday _____

15. Mister _____

16. tablespoon _____

17. circle _____

18. company _____

Day 17

Choose 4 <u>compound words</u> and illustrate them.
EXAMPLE: <u>drawbridge</u> is <u>draw</u> and <u>bridge</u>.
Here are some to choose from or you can choose some of your own: billfold, screwdriver, backyard, butterfly, rainbow, mushroom, supermarket, post-man, undertake, windpipe, starfish, basketball.

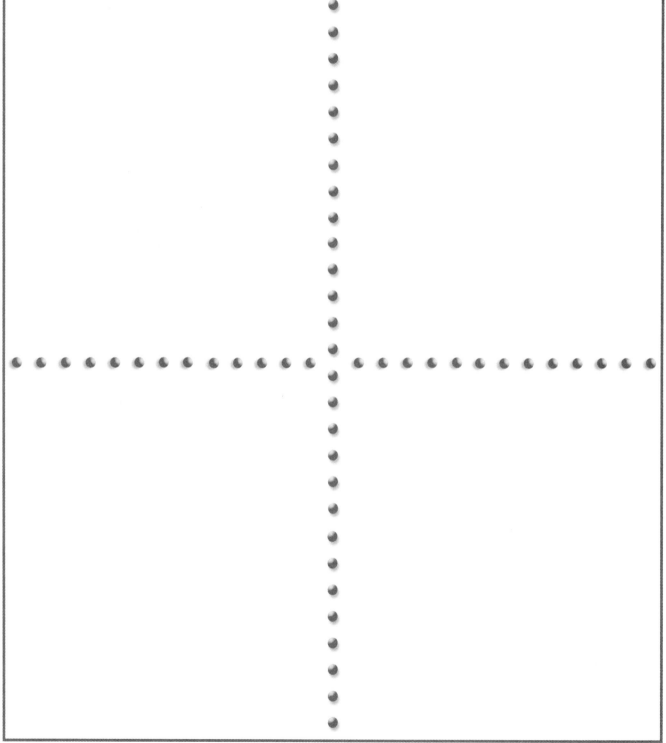

Understanding polygons.

Closed figures that have straight lines are *polygons*.
Which of these are polygons?_____

1.　　　　2.　　　　3.　　　　4.　　　　5.

Why? _____

Where each side or point meets is called a *vertex*. Count and write the number
of sides and the number of vertices each polygon has.

triangle	pentagon	quadrilateral	octagon
sides _____	sides _____	sides _____	sides _____
vertices _____	vertices _____	vertices _____	vertices _____

How are these shapes below alike? _____

How are they different? _____

Write the book titles correctly. <u>Remember:</u> **Underline the whole title and
use capital letters at the beginning of all the important words and the last
word in the title.**

1. millions of cats　_____

2. higher than the arrow　_____

3. john paul jones　_____

4. no flying in the house　_____

5. ludo and the star horse　_____

6. marvin k. money, will you please leave now?

_____

7. an elephant is not a cat　_____

8. one wide river to cross　_____

9. the polar express　_____

10. where the sidewalk ends　_____

Day 18

Neighborhood Survey. **Conduct a survey with your neighborhood, friends, or relatives. Find out how many have pets. If possible, observe them with their pets. Do they keep their pets inside or outside? Are the pets left to find their own food, part of their food, or is their food provided for them? How much space do they have to move around in? What are the conditions of their pets? Think of other questions you might ask. Record your information either in a report, chart, graph, table, or a picture.**

Use what you know about polygons to make a pattern. Start with one polygon and flip, turn, or slide it to make a pattern.

EXAMPLE:

or

Now try your hand at making some polygon patterns.

Review of Homonyms or Homophones. **Write 10 sentences using some of these pairs of homonyms or homophones. Be sure to use both words and underline the homonyms you use.**

EXAMPLE: <u>Would</u> you chop some <u>wood</u>?

1. no, know	**7.** sun, son	**13.** rode, road
2. ate, eight	**8.** tail, tale	**14.** pair, pear
3. see, sea	**9.** sale, sail	**15.** their, there
4. knight, night	**10.** so, sew	**16.** hour, our
5. new, knew	**11.** way, weigh	**17.** red, read
6. four, for	**12.** sent, cent	**18.** wear, where

_____

_____

_____

_____

_____

_____

_____

_____

_____

_____

Read this paragraph. Put in the punctuation marks that are missing. Don't forget capitals.

do you ever wonder about the planet pluto it takes pluto 248 earth years to orbit the sun most of the time pluto is farther away from the sun than any other planet but for some time pluto had been closer to the sun than neptune because it was traveling inside neptune's orbit it remained in neptunes orbit until february 9 1999 pluto is now traveling out of neptunes orbit

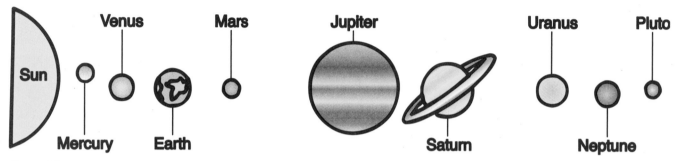

See if you can find more information about Pluto. Did you know that some astronomers believe that it was once a moon of Neptune? Look in an encyclopedia to find out more.

Chart the weather and temperature for the month. You will need to check with the weatherman for the high and low temperatures for the day. Write down or draw the weather for the day. Include the high and low temperature.

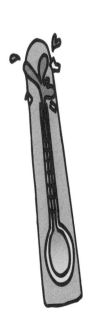

Sun.	Mon.	Tues.	Weds.	Thurs.	Fri.	Sat.

Rename these fractions. The first one is done for you.

1. $\frac{5}{4}$ = $1\frac{1}{4}$
2. $\frac{10}{3}$ =
3. $\frac{9}{8}$ =
4. $\frac{8}{3}$ =

5. $\frac{5}{2}$ =
6. $\frac{7}{4}$ =
7. $\frac{10}{3}$ =
8. $\frac{11}{10}$ =

9. $\frac{10}{7}$ =
10. $\frac{19}{8}$ =
11. $\frac{25}{10}$ =
12. $\frac{9}{5}$ =

13. $\frac{31}{10}$ =
14. $\frac{23}{10}$ =
15. $\frac{17}{8}$ =
16. $\frac{13}{3}$ =

17. $\frac{25}{12}$ =
18. $\frac{28}{9}$ =
19. $\frac{36}{10}$ =
20. $\frac{9}{4}$ =

21. $\frac{13}{6}$ =
22. $\frac{215}{100}$ =
23. $\frac{76}{25}$ =
24. $\frac{100}{3}$ =

Name the parts of a letter.

1 _____

2 _____

3 _____

4 _____

5 _____

1 1624 Oak Avenue
Amarillo, TX 79103
June 20, 1995

2 Dear Patt,

3 Today my friends and I went swimming in June's pool. We had a lot of fun.

I sure miss you. I wish your family hadn't moved. Have you made any new friends yet?

Please write to me as soon as you can.

4 Your friend,

5 Judy

Complete each sentence by circling the word that is spelled correctly, then write it in the blank space. Use a dictionary if necessary.

1. The big cat couldn't _____ from the trap.
   a. escape   b. iscape   c. eskape   d. acape   e. iccape

2. Mother paid $100.00 for _____.
   a. groseries   b. groceeries   c. groceries   d. grcerees   e. grooseries

3. Anna is a very _____ person.
   a. kreative   b. creative   c. createive   d. crative   e. creetive

4. Have you ever seen a more _____ man?
   a. handsum   b. hansome   c. handsume   d. handcome   e. handsome

5. We love to _____ ride in the winter.
   a. sleigh   b. sleia   c. cleigh   d. slagh   e. sleeigh

6. I found the perfect _____ for my new dress.
   a. matterial   b. matirial   c. metariel   d. material   e. materiall

7. Scott's son got a _____ to Harvard University.
   a. schoolarship   b. scholarship   c. skullarship   d. sholarship   e. scholership

8. What would it take to _____ your appetite?
   a. satesfy   b. satisfi   c. satisffy   d. catisfy   e. satisfy

9. Richard, turn down the _____!
   a. volime   b. volumee   c. volume   d. volumme   e. valume

10. That was a _____ report, Amy.
    a. fantistic   b. fantastik   c. fanntastic   d. fantastic   e. fantestic

11. We saw a man fight an _____ in the show.
    a. aligator   b. alligator   c. allegator   d. alligetor   e. alligater

12. Do you understand the _____?
    a. instructions   b. enstructions   c. instiructions   d. instrucions   e. instracteons

Electricity. **Make a list of all the things around you that use electricity.**

_____

_____

_____

_____

_____

_____

_____

_____

_____

_____

_____

Words to Sound, Read, and Spell

ability
capability

accept
except

adapt
adept
adopt

adjoin
adjourn

advice
advise

affect
effect

aid
aide

air
heir

all right
alright

all together
altogether

allusion
illusion

although
though

appraise
apprise

arms
alms

ascent
assent

assay
essay

averse
adverse

bases
basis

beau
bough
bow

bell
belle

beside
besides

born
borne

bullion
bouillon

breach
breech

calendar
calender

callous
callus

cannon
canon

canvass
canvas

capital
capitol

casual
causal

sensor
censure

cents
scents
sense

cession
session

charted
charter

choral
coral
corral

cite
sight
site

clench
clinch

flick
clique

coarse
course

complement
compliment

compose
comprise

confidant
confident

core
corps

council
counsel

continual
continuous

coward
cowered

currant
current

decree
degree

defer
differ

descent
dissent

desert
dessert

distract
detract

emigrate
immigrate

eminent
imminent

ensure
insure

envelop
envelope

errand
errant

exalt
exult

extant
extent

fair
fare

farther
further

feint
faint

flair
flare

flew
flu
flue

flounder
founder

flout
flaunt

foreword
forward

formally
formerly

frees
freeze
frieze

gait
gate

grate
great

grisly
gristly
grizzly

hail
hale

hallow
hollow

hangar
hanger

hoard
horde

hoarse
horse

Words to Sound, Read, and Spell

hospitable
hospital

idle
idol

incite
insight

intense
intents

interstate
intrastate
intestate

its
it's

jam
jamb

key
quay
cay

kneed
need

knight
night

later
latter

lay
lie

lean
lien

leave
let

lend
loan

liable
libel

load
lode

loath
loathe

lose
loose

main
mane

manner
manor

mantel
mantle

maybe
may be

medal
mettle

moat
mote

morning
mourning

naval
navel

ordinance
ordnance

pail
pale

pain
pane

palate
palette
pallet

passed
past

peak
peek
pique

peddle
pedal

peer
pier

personal
personnel

plane
plain

pole
pull

pore
pour
poor

pray
prey

prescribe
proscribe

pretense
pretext

rain
reign
rein

raise
raze

respectfully
respectively

role
roll

root
route

sail
sale

set
sit

shear
sheer

sloe
slough
slow

soar
sore

speciality
specialty

stationary
stationery

straight
strait

tail
tale

team
teem

tear
tier

tenant
tenet

then
than

their
there
they're

tic
tick

timber
timbre

track
tract

vail
vale

vain
vane

vial
vile

waive
wave

weather
whether

were
was

wet
whet

whither
wither

who
whom

who's
whose

wrack
rack

wrest
rest

Summer Bridge Activities™
Incentive Contract Calendar

Month _____

My parents and I decided that if I complete 15 days of
Summer Bridge Activities™ and read _____ minutes a day,
my incentive/reward will be:

_____

Child's Signature _____
Parent's Signature _____

Day 1   📖 ⭐ ——

Day 2   📖 ⭐ ——

Day 3   📖 ⭐ ——

Day 4   📖 ⭐ ——

Day 5   📖 ⭐ ——

Day 6   📖 ⭐ ——

Day 7   📖 ⭐ ——

Day 8   📖 ⭐ ——

Day 9   📖 ⭐ ——

Day 10   📖 ⭐ ——

Day 11   📖 ⭐ ——

Day 12   📖 ⭐ ——

Day 13   📖 ⭐ ——

Day 14   📖 ⭐ ——

Day 15   📖 ⭐ ——

Child: Color the ⭐ for daily activities completed.
Color the 📖 for daily reading completed.

Parent: Initial the _____ for daily activities and reading
your child completes.

Fun Activity Ideas to Go Along with the Third Section!

1. Draw a picture of your favorite friend, toy, or teacher during your favorite time of the year.

2. Put together a collection of leaves from your neighborhood and label as many as you can.

3. Write five questions that you would like to ask the President of the United States.

4. Invent a new ice cream flavor. How is it made? What will you call it?

5. Play football with a frisbee.

6. Find out how to recycle in your town, then make and deliver flyers to inform all your neighbors.

7. Using a book on astronomy, look for stars and constellations. This is a fun nighttime activity.

8. Write your answer to the following question: How would the world be different without Alexander Graham Bell?

9. Surprise your parents and weed a flower bed or garden, rake the leaves, do the dishes, etc.

10. Play flashlight tag, tonight!

11. Design a comic strip and draw it.

12. Paint a mural on butcher paper.

13. Pretend you live in the year 2028. How will life be different? How will you look? What will you eat? How will you get around? Write it down and draw it.

14. Set up a miniature golf course in your own backyard.

15. Play hockey using a broom.

Adding and remaining fractions where needed. The first one is done for you.

1. $\dfrac{3}{4} + \dfrac{2}{4} = \dfrac{5}{4}$ or $1\dfrac{1}{4}$

2. $\dfrac{9}{11} + \dfrac{2}{11} =$

3. $\dfrac{7}{12} + \dfrac{8}{12} =$

4. $\dfrac{9}{16} + \dfrac{9}{16} =$

5. $\dfrac{6}{10} + \dfrac{8}{10} =$

6. $\dfrac{10}{12} + \dfrac{14}{12} =$

7. $\dfrac{5}{10} + \dfrac{6}{10} =$

8. $\dfrac{12}{24} + \dfrac{13}{24} =$

9. $\dfrac{6}{8} + \dfrac{5}{8} =$

10. $\dfrac{4}{7} + \dfrac{5}{7} =$

11. $\dfrac{3}{4} + \dfrac{5}{4} =$

12. $\dfrac{6}{11} + \dfrac{7}{11} =$

13. $\dfrac{5}{15} + \dfrac{10}{15} =$

14. $\dfrac{8}{9} + \dfrac{6}{9} =$

15. $\dfrac{10}{16} + \dfrac{9}{16} =$

16. $\dfrac{15}{20} + \dfrac{15}{20} =$

Look at the the letter on page 75 to answer the following questions.

1. What does the heading tell you?_____

_____

2. How many paragraphs are in the letter? _____

3. What is the signature?_____

_____

4. What words in the letter have capitals? _____

_____

_____

5. Where are the commas in the letter? _____

_____

_____

_____

Electric Circuit Crossword Puzzle.

Across

1. Electric currents from a battery flow in one direction from
   n __ __ __ __ __ __ __ to p __ __ __ __ __ __ __.
2. Electrical c __ __ __ __ __ __ means going around in a circle arriving back
   where it started.
3. M __ __ __ __ __ are good conductors of electrical currents because electricity can flow through them easily.
4. The plastic or rubber covering on wires is called I __ __ __ __ __ __ __ __ __ __.
5. In a lightbulb, when the switch is turned on or connected, the electricity flows
   through what we call a c __ __ __ __ __ __ c __ __ __ __ __ __.
6. When electricity flows through the wires on a toaster they become hot and
   h __ __ __ from the wires toasts our bread.
7. L __ __ __ __ __ and thickness are the two things that determine the wires'
   resistance that causes them to become hot.
8. A __ __ __ __ __ __ __ __ __ __ such as electric stoves and toasters contain
   wires that are conductors of electricity.
9. A b __ __ __ __ __ __ is a cell storing an electrical charge and capable of fur-
   nishing an electrical current.
10. Copper and aluminum are good c __ __ __ __ __ __ __ __ __ __ of electricity
    because electricity can go through them easily, due to their low resistance to
    the electrical current.

Down

1. A r __ __ __ __ __ __ __ __ __ is a
   tool used to control the
   amount of electrical current
   that goes through a circuit.
2. When wires, bulbs, and batteries are connected they
   make a path for electricity to
   flow through called an
   e __ __ __ __ __ __ __ __ __
   c __ __ __ __ __ __ __.
3. Lightbulbs have a special wire
   in them called a
   f __ __ __ __ __ __ __.
4. The property of the filament
   that makes it light up when
   electricity flows through it is
   called the
   r __ __ __ __ __ __ __ __ __ __
   to electricity.

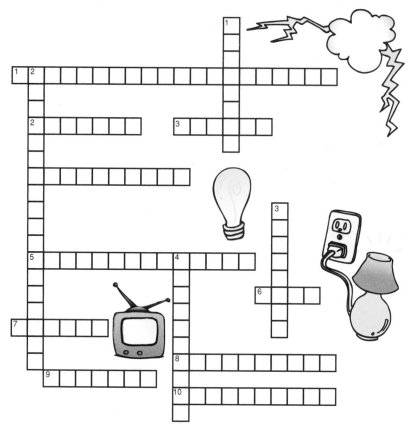

Subtracting fractions.

$$\frac{4}{5} - \frac{1}{5} = \frac{3}{5}$$ ← Subtract the numerators.
← Keep the same denominators.

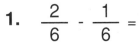

1. $\frac{2}{6} - \frac{1}{6} =$

2. $\frac{6}{8} - \frac{3}{8} =$

3. $\frac{11}{12} - \frac{7}{12} =$

4. $\frac{5}{10} - \frac{3}{10} =$

5. $\frac{8}{11} - \frac{3}{11} =$

6. $\frac{4}{5} - \frac{1}{5} =$

7. $\frac{3}{4} - \frac{2}{4} =$

8. $\frac{6}{7} - \frac{4}{7} =$

9. $\frac{5}{9} - \frac{2}{9} =$

10. $6\frac{8}{10}$
$-\ 3\frac{4}{10}$
_____

11. $8\frac{4}{10}$
$-\ 3\frac{3}{10}$
_____

12. $7\frac{2}{5}$
$-\ 3\frac{1}{5}$
_____

13. $6\frac{7}{8}$
$-\ 3\frac{4}{8}$
_____

14. $13\frac{3}{4}$
$-\ 9\frac{1}{4}$
_____

15. $14\frac{10}{12}$
$-\ 7\frac{9}{12}$
_____

16. $24\frac{7}{10}$
$-\ 12\frac{3}{10}$
_____

17. $15\frac{8}{9}$
$-\ 7\frac{3}{9}$
_____

Put all the punctuation marks and capital letters in this letter.

Mr. Greg Jones
1461 Condor St.
Lake Tona, OH

1461 condor st
lake tona oh
july 21 1995

dear david

thank you for sending me the pictures of your trip it looks like you had a great time do you want me to send them back

next week im going to kansas city to spend the rest of the summer with my dad i hope we will get along well

write again when you can

your friend

greg

Body Facts. **Use the words in the Word Box to complete these sentences on "Body Facts."**

1. Our body is made up of millions of tiny _____.

2. Our body is mostly _____; between 55 and 75 percent.

3. Our body has lots of metals and minerals in it, some of which are _____ and _____.

4. Our bodies have several systems that work together to help us. Our heart, blood vessels, and blood are part of our _____ system to move blood throughout our bodies.

5. Our salivary glands, esophagus, stomach, gallbladder, large intestines, and small intestines are part of our _____ system.

6. Our _____ is like a wonderful tool. It tells our _____ to beat and our _____ to blink.

Word Box

- brain
- water
- calcium
- circulatory
- cells
- iron
- digestive
- eyes
- heart

Our Five Senses Can Sense Danger! **Think about your five senses—touch, smell, sight, hearing, and taste. Now list all the ways your five senses can protect you or keep you from danger. Which sense do you trust most to keep you from danger?**

_____

_____

_____

_____

_____

_____

_____

_____

_____

_____

_____

Addition and Subtraction with Thousands

1. 5,162
   - 2,678

2. 9,252
   - 5,003

3. 7,825
   - 3,148

4. 3,529
   + 7,506

5. 8,929
   + 4,050

6. 9,341
   - 6,037

7. 2,629
   + 7,536

8. 4,528
   + 1,257

9. 7,932
   - 5,847

10. 9,826
    + 1,329

11. 4,723
    + 5,297

12. 3,872
    - 1,799

13. 8,000
    - 4,587

14. 7,909
    + 5,360

15. 9,031
    - 5,592

16. 2,354
    + 5,967

Write a letter to a friend, grandparent, or someone else you would like to write. Be sure to put in all five parts of the letter. **Remember:** Letter writing uses the same steps as writing a story. Refer to page 9. Copy it to another sheet of paper.

Below are the stressed syllables of some spelling words. Write the other syllables and then write the words in cursive. Each blank stands for a letter. The first one is done for you.

favor	amount	busy	accept	violin
paddle	piano	begin	dial	bacon
several	salad	wonderful	unlock	vegetable
~~parent~~	library	limit	into	depend

1. par´ _ent_   _parent_
2. li´ _ _ _ _ _   _____
3. lim´ _ _   _____
4. in´ _ _   _____
5. _ _ pend´   _____
6. ba´ _ _ _   _____
7. di´ _ _   _____
8. _ _ gin´   _____
9. pi´ _ _ _   _____
10. pad´ _ _ _   _____
11. sev´ _ _ _ _   _____
12. sal´ _ _   _____
13. won´ _ _ _ _ _ _   _____
14. _ _ lock´   _____
15. veg´ _ _ _ _ _ _   _____
16. _ _ _ lin´   _____
17. _ _ cept´   _____
18. bus´ _   _____
19. _ mount´   _____
20. fa´ _ _ _   _____

Self-Portrait Poem.

1. Write your name.
2. Write two words that tell about you.
3. Write three words that tell what you like to do.
4. Write two more words that describe you.
5. Write your name again.

Try writing another "portrait poem" about a favorite person or pet in your life.

_____   _____
_____   _____
_____   _____
_____   _____
_____   _____
_____   _____
_____   _____

It's About Time! <u>Remember:</u> There are 24 hours in a day. The times from midnight to noon are written a.m. and the times from noon to midnight are written p.m. Write down the times. Remember a.m. and p.m.

1. _____

2. _____

3. _____

4. Write the time 50 minutes later than clock 1. _____

5. Write the time 25 minutes earlier than clock 2. _____

6. Write the time 95 minutes later than clock 3. _____

7. How much earlier is clock 1 than clock 2? _____

8. How much later is clock 3 than clock 2? _____

9. Add 12 hours to clock 1 and what time is it? _____

10. What was the time 6 hours before clock 2? _____

This envelope is not addressed correctly. Rewrite it correctly. <u>Remember:</u> The <u>return</u> <u>address</u> is the address of the person writing the letter, and the <u>address</u> is the address of the person to whom the letter is going.

1461 condor st
mr greg jones
lake tona oh

mr david fisher
little creek id
route 2 box 3 f

_____
_____
_____

_____
_____

Who Did It?

Grayson and Tanner were playing baseball in their backyard with some friends. They had been playing all afternoon in the hot sun.

Tanner decided that he was tired of playing ball. He sat down on the back steps to watch the others play. "Man, am I thirsty," said Tanner. "I'm going in the house to get a drink." Several of the others decided that they were thirsty and went inside with Tanner. "Wait for me!" hollered Grayson. "I'm coming, too!"

The boys agreed to watch television instead of playing more baseball. Then the guys thought they had better go home, because it was close to dinnertime. Grayson said he was hungry and was going to look in the kitchen for something to eat. Tanner ran after him to remind him that their mom said they were not to eat anything before dinner. About that time their mother came into the kitchen to fix dinner. "Who ate all the hot dogs?" she exclaimed. "They were right here on the counter." Grayson and Tanner looked at each other. "Not us, Mom," they said. "Somebody must have. Do you have any clues?" They both agreed that it wasn't either one of them and that it couldn't have been their friends, because they were all there together.

They started looking around for clues to discover what happened. The mud off their shoes had left tracks on the floor, but had come nowhere near where Mother had put the hot dogs. After their survey of the kitchen, they sat down to discuss the "case of the missing hot dogs." Then they heard what sounded like a satisfied meow from the den. The three of them walked into the den to find Tiger, their cat, finishing off the last hot dog. He licked both his paws clean and meowed loudly. "No wonder we didn't find any cat tracks in the kitchen where the hot dogs were," laughed Mother. "Tiger always keeps his paws very clean, unlike some boys I know."

After reading this story, write down at least five things you know about Tanner and Grayson.

1._____

_____

2._____

_____

3._____

_____

4._____

_____

5._____

_____

Fractions to Tenths and the Decimal Equivalents for the Fraction.
<u>Remember</u>: **When working with fractions that have a denominator of 10, you can write them as fractions in tenths, or you can use the decimal equivalent. Do this activity by writing each both ways.**

1. [bar] $\frac{6}{10}$ or <u>.6</u>   7. $\frac{3}{10}$ or ___.___

2. [bar] ___ or ___   8. $1\frac{7}{10}$ or ___.___

3. [bar] ___ or ___   9. $3\frac{5}{10}$ or ___.___

4. [bar] ___ or ___   10. 1.9 or _____

5. [bar] ___ or ___   11. .8 or _____

6. [bar] ___ or ___   12. 3.4 or _____

On page 85, you wrote a letter to someone. Today, address an envelope and send the letter to them. Be sure to put your address in the upper left-hand corner and the address of the person to whom you're sending the letter in the center. Don't forget to put a stamp in the upper right-hand corner. Use the space below to practice.

Write an analogy to finish these sentences. <u>Remember:</u> An analogy is a comparison between two pairs of words. Try to think of the relationship between the two words given and then think of another word that has the same kind of relationship to the third word.

EXAMPLE: <u>Story</u> is to <u>read</u> as <u>song</u> is to <u>sing</u>.

1. Brother is to boy as sister is to _____.
2. Princess is to queen as prince is to _____.
3. Milk is to drink as hamburger is to _____.
4. Arrow is to bow as bullet is to _____.
5. Car is to driver as plane is to _____.
6. Ceiling is to room as lid is to _____.
7. Paper is to tear as glass is to _____.
8. Large is to huge as small is to _____.
9. Wrist is to hand as ankle is to _____.
10. Father is to uncle as mother is to _____.
11. Cupboard is to dishes as library is to _____.
12. Hard is to difficult as easy is to _____.
13. Moon is to earth as earth is to _____.
14. Time is to clock as date is to _____.

Exercising Parts of the Body. **Make a list of 5 or 6 exercises. Some examples are running, hopping, sit-ups, jumping jacks, touching your toes, push-ups, jumping, skipping, playing sports, gymnastics, and swinging your arms. Try them. Which parts of the body are affected? Write down the results. Try this exercise. Take an ordinary spring-centered clothespin. Hold the ends between your thumb and one of your fingers. How many times can you open and close it in 30 to 40 seconds?**

_____

_____

_____

_____

_____

_____

_____

Use what you know about <u>fractions</u> <u>to</u> <u>tenths</u> and their <u>decimal</u> equivalents to work with <u>hundreds</u>. **Remember:** When a whole object is divided into 100 equal parts, each part is <u>one</u> hundredth (¹⁄₁₀₀ or .01). Write the fraction as a decimal. The first one is done for you.

1. $\frac{49}{100}$ = .49

2. $\frac{25}{100}$ = .___

3. $\frac{20}{100}$ = .___

4. $\frac{52}{100}$ = .___

5. $\frac{86}{100}$ = .___

6. $\frac{37}{100}$ = .___

7. $\frac{4}{100}$ = .___

8. $\frac{9}{100}$ = .___

Now write the mixed number as a decimal.

9. $1\frac{93}{100}$ = __.__

10. $7\frac{15}{100}$ = __.__

11. $9\frac{13}{100}$ = __.__

12. $15\frac{47}{100}$ = __.__

13. $46\frac{89}{100}$ = __.__

14. $35\frac{6}{100}$ = __.__

15. $94\frac{7}{100}$ = __.__

16. $625\frac{12}{100}$ = __.__

17. $12\frac{5}{100}$ = __.__

18. $81\frac{1}{100}$ = __.__

19. $37\frac{87}{100}$ = __.__

20. $10\frac{11}{100}$ = __.__

Adjectives are words that tell about or describe nouns and pronouns. Circle the adjective(s) in these sentences. Write the noun(s) or pronoun(s) that it describes at the end of the sentence. The first one is done for you.

1. A (beautiful) light flashed across the (cloudy) sky. *light   sky*

2. Her golden hair was very long. _____

3. On the tall mountain we found blue and yellow flowers. _____

_____

4. He was brave after the accident. _____

5. It is fun, but it is also dangerous to skydive. _____

6. Our brown dog had six cute puppies. _____

_____

Now fill in the blanks with adjectives.

7. My _____ pencil is never in my desk.

8. The _____ students were having a _____ time.

9. Lions are _____ animals that we can see in the zoo.

10. The _____, _____ ride was making me sick.

11. My brother, Jack, sang a _____ song when we were camping.

12. _____, _____ snakes were wiggling around in the box.

Maintaining Good Health. **Match the following health terms —**
nutrients, healthy, sleep, exercise, liquids or water, cleanliness,
checkups, energy, food groups.

1. _____ are basic nourishing ingredients in good foods that we eat.
2. _____ helps us to strengthen our muscles. It helps our heart and lungs grow, too.
3. _____ help find methods of preventing tooth decay and maintaining good health.
4. Meat, fruit and vegetables, milk, breads, and cereals make up the basic four _____ _____ that keep us healthy.
5. Being healthy means feeling good and having the _____ to work and play.
6. Vitamins and minerals are kinds of _____ that we get from food.
7. Being _____ means feeling good and not being sick.
8. Sugar, starch, and fats are _____ that the body uses for fuel to give us _____.
9. We need to drink a lot of _____ because our body is approximately 80 percent _____.
10. Plenty of _____ helps give our body time to grow and repair itself. Children need 10 to 11 hours of it because they are not finished growing.
11. _____ is a way of fighting germs and staying healthy.
12. We need health _____ by a doctor or dentist at least once a year.

Are you confused?

1. Are any of the lines curved?

_____

2. Which line is the longest?

_____

3. Which vase is wider at the top and bottom? _____

4. Which line is the longer, a or b?

_____

5. Is the hat taller than it is wide? _____

Decimals and Money. <u>Remember</u>: 100 pennies = 1 dollar. One penny is 1/100 of a dollar or $.01, so 49 pennies = $.49. We can compute money by adding, subtracting, multiplying, and dividing — just watch the decimals. Look at the signs. Use a separate piece of paper to show your work.

EXAMPLE:

```
  $57.34          $62.89          $12.45              $3.95
 +62.89          -34.91          x    3          5 ) $19.75
 ------          ------          ------              -15
 $20.23          $27.98          $37.35               47
                                                     -45
                                                      25
                                                     -25
                                                       0
```

1. $409.75
   - 249.83
   $.

2. $14.74
   x   3
   $.

3. $492.00
   - 349.50
   $.

4. $.
4) $12.92

5. $162.49
   + 186.32
   $.

6. 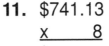 $.
7) $49.77

7. $601.89
   + 403.23
   $.

8. $9.57
   x 6
  $.

9. $668.45
   + 171.63
   $.

10. $915.04
   - 102.56
   $.

11. $741.13
   x   8
   $.

12. $.
4) $29.48

Write nouns to go with these adjectives. The first one is done for you.

1. two, red *apples*
2. fluffy, yellow _____
3. cold, wet _____
4. dark, strange _____
5. wild, dangerous _____
6. black, furry _____
7. big, heavy _____
8. fancy, little _____

9. pink, small _____
10. smooth, green _____
11. fat, juicy _____
12. loud, shrill _____
13. fourteen, blue _____
14. long, thick _____
15. cozy, warm _____
16. sharp, silver _____

Add a prefix and a suffix to the following words, then choose five of the words and write a sentence with them.

prefix

suffix

1. _____ print _____   7. _____ lock _____
2. _____ light _____   8. _____ port _____
3. _____ poison _____   9. _____ cook _____
4. _____ courage_____   10. _____ appoint _____
5. _____ agree _____   11. _____ record _____
6. _____ spell _____   12. _____ health _____

Sentences:

1. _____
_____

2. _____
_____

3. _____
_____

4. _____
_____

5. _____
_____

What's for Breakfast, Lunch, and Dinner? **This is your day to plan the meals. You can have anything you want to eat for the day. It can be for the whole family or just yourself. Plan and write down your menu for breakfast, lunch, and dinner. You can even schedule a few snacks.**

_____
_____
_____
_____
_____
_____
_____
_____

Multiplying Multiples of 10 and 100.

10 x 8 = 80	10 x 80 = 800	10 x 800 = 8,000

In order to use shortcuts to find the product of multiples of 10 or 100 write the product for the basic fact, and count the zeros in the factors.

Multiples of tens:

1. 10 x 5 = _____
2. 7 x 10 = _____
3. 39 x 10 = _____
4. 30 x 30 = _____
5. 54 x 10 = _____
6. 10 x 21 = _____
7. 710 x 10 = _____
8. 9 x 10 = _____
9. 70 x 30 = _____
10. 40 x 40 = _____
11. 85 x 10 = _____
12. 341 x 10 = _____

Multiples of hundreds:

13. 900
    x 40

14. 600
    x 10

15. 230
    x 20

16. 700
    x 80

17. 500
    x 50

18. 600
    x 90

19. 440
    x30

20. 700
    x 60

Adjectives can be used to compare. Write these adjectives. Add -er and -est.

EXAMPLE: red _____ *redder* _____ *reddest* _____

1. hot _____ _____ _____
2. nice _____ _____ _____
3. warm _____ _____ _____
4. hard _____ _____ _____
5. easy _____ _____ _____
6. few _____ _____ _____

Now write a story. Use as many of the adjectives above as you can. Underline the adjectives.

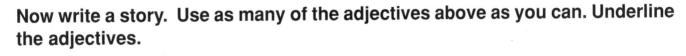

_____

_____

_____

_____

_____

Day 8

Idioms. Choose four <u>idioms and illustrate them.</u> Here are some to choose from or you can use your own.

- Lend a hand.
- She's a ball of fire.
- He's got rocks in his head.
- She gave him a dirty look.
- I got it straight from the horse's mouth.
- You won the game by the skin of your teeth.

- Time flies.
- Keep a stiff upper lip.
- The boys were shooting the breeze.
- I'd really like to catch her eye.
- I was dog tired.

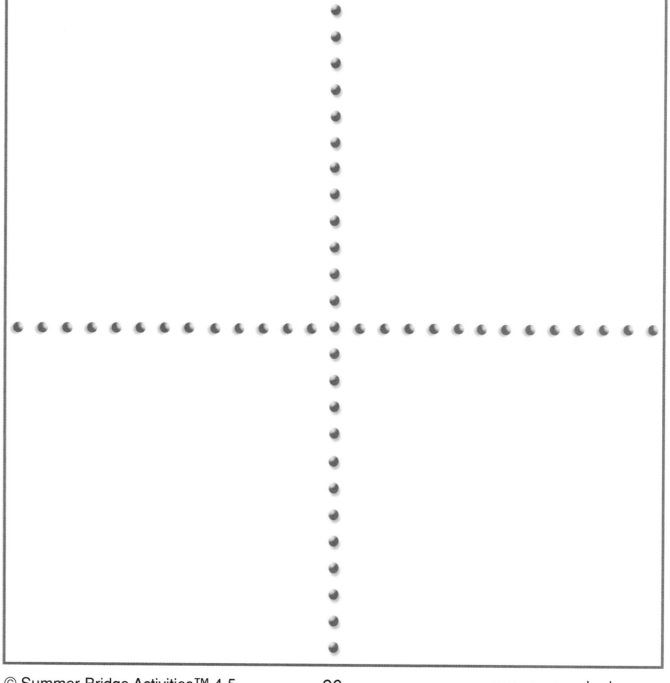

Place-Value. **A place-value chart can help us read as well as figure out large numbers.**

Hundred Millions	Ten Millions	Millions	Hundred Thousands	Ten Thousands	Thousands	Hundreds	Tens	Ones
8	6	5	3	7	1	4	3	

Using the place-value chart to help you, read and write the following numbers. The first one is done for you

1. Eighty-six million, five hundred thirty-seven thousand, one hundred forty-three

   __86,537,143__ .

2. Seven hundred eighty-nine million, four hundred ninety-six thousand, three hundred twenty-one _____ .

3. One hundred sixty million, seven hundred six thousand, one hundred, twenty-nine

   _____ .

4. Seventy-one million, four hundred eleven thousand, eight hundred ninety-nine

   _____ .

5. One hundred million, three hundred seventy-five thousand _____ .

6. Ninety million, two hundred fifty-seven thousand, four hundred forty-three

   _____ .

7.   1,369,000 _____

8. 375,403,101 _____

9. 894,336,045 _____

10. 284,300,070 _____

Overworked And. **Rewrite the paragraph and leave out all the occurrences of and that you can. Write in cursive and be sure to put capitals and periods where they need to go.**

My friend and I visited Cardiff, Wales and we learned that Cardiff is the capital and largest port of Wales and the city lies on the River Taff near the Bristol Channel and Cardiff is near the largest coal mines in Great Britain and it is one of the great coal-shipping ports of the world.

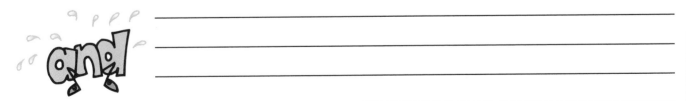

_____

_____

_____

_____

How many times were you able to leave and out of the paragraph?_____

The following words are often misspelled. Write each word three times, then have someone give you a test. Use another piece of paper for your test.

EXAMPLE:

1. although _*although*   *although*   *although*_
2. arithmetic _____
3. trouble _____
4. bought _____
5. chocolate _____
6. aunt _____
7. handkerchief _____
8. piece _____
9. vacation _____
10. practice _____
11. receive _____
12. getting _____
13. lessons _____
14. weather _____
15. surprise _____

YOUR
Test
Score

Categorizing the People in Your Family. Include some aunts, uncles, and cousins. Categorize them according to age, height, weight, hair color, hair length, eye color, etc. What do they have in common? What are some of their differences? Then draw a picture of them. Use another sheet of paper.

Family member	age	height	weight	hair color

1. 39	2. 72	3. 85	4. 23
x 69	x 18	x 36	x 87

5. 46	6. 57	7. 41	8. 48	9. 88
x 77	x 49	x 73	x 95	x 66

10. 68	11. 507	12. 456	13. 640	14. 576
x 92	x 13	x 32	x 21	x 45

Write <u>S</u> behind the word pairs that are synonyms, <u>A</u> for antonyms, or <u>H</u> for homonyms.

EXAMPLE:

ties • bind **S**

high • low **A**

here • hear **H**

1. weep • cry ____

2. wonderful • terrible ____

3. look • glare ____

4. huge • large ____

5. away • toward ____

6. walk • stroll ____

7. never • always ____

8. bear • bare ____

9. ask • told ____

10. cymbal • symbol ____

11. many • numerous ____

12. end • begin ____

13. hair • hare ____

14. move • transport ____

15. problem • solution ____

16. idea • thought ____

17. claws • clause ____

18. I'll • isle ____

19. add • subtract ____

20. try • attempt ____

21. that • this ____

22. doe • dough ____

23. enough • ample ____

24. board • bored ____

25. day • date ____

26. capital • capitol ____

27. leave • arrive ____

Do this crossword puzzle. Read the clues to help you decide what words go in the boxes. Dark lines mark the end of words.

Down

1. won't bend easily
3. nothing in it
4. another name for a mule
7. boards for building
9. gave money
10. red from the sun
13. very large; great
14. eat outside

Across

2. frilly
5. beginning of a word
6. hair by the eye
8. do it again to a story
11. plays the piano
12. holds up the gate
15. decay of food
16. cook in
17. birds with webbed feet

Finish drawing the illusion. Is it a face or a vase? It's both! (Look until you see them.)

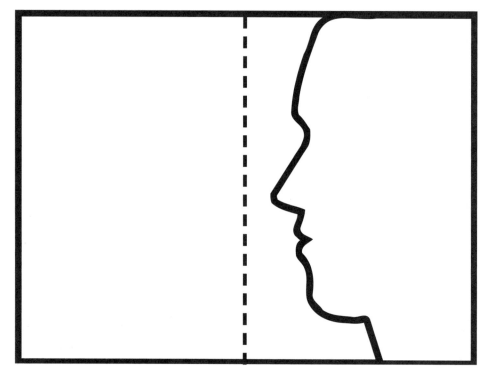

Quotients with Remainders. **Use another sheet of paper.**

EXAMPLE:

```
      2 R8
1.  20) 48
        40
         8
```

2. 30) 189

3. 70) 456

4. 80) 504

5. 30) 281

6. 60) 246

7. 90) 458

8. 60) 573

9. 40) 172

10. 30) 216

11. 30) 121

12. 90) 500

13. 80) 410

12. 60) 692

15. 70) 661

Think of one of your favorite fairy tales. Tell how the story begins, what happens in the middle, and how it ends. Write it in your own words and in the correct order. Don't write the whole story.

Categorize these words and tell why they go in the same category. You put the headings in this time.

deciliter	program	kindness	remorse	drugs
quart	poison	yard	hate	acre
anger	software	jealousy	Fahrenheit	joystick
alcohol	Celsius	liter	ton	gram
ounce	disk	mouse	cursor	meter
marijuana	caffeine	tobacco	kilogram	fear

1.	2.	3.	4.	5.

Tell why. Because they all...

1. _____
2. _____
3. _____
4. _____
5. _____

Make a "Love" list and then a "Hate" list. Put the things you love most at the top of your list. Do the same thing with your "Hate" list.

Love List

Hate List

_____ | _____
_____ | _____
_____ | _____
_____ | _____
_____ | _____
_____ | _____

Multiplying Money. <u>Remember:</u> **Multiply as you do using whole numbers and then place the decimal point or cents (2 numbers from the right). Use another sheet of paper to show your work.**

EXAMPLE:

```
    $.24        24   x       9    =    216
   x 89         24   x      80    =   1920
    216       1920   +     216    =   2136
  +1920       Place the decimal and the dollar sign
   2136       $21.36
```

1. $.65 x 24	2. $.52 x 36	3. $.94 x 13	4. $.45 x 25
5. $.81 x 34	6. $.59 x 54	7. $.75 x 22	8. $.98 x 34
9. $3.45 x 56	10. $3.52 x 34	11. $5.75 x 24	12. $8.93 x 73

Adverbs Describe Verbs. **Write an adverb to describe these verbs.**
<u>Remember:</u> **Many adverbs end with -ly. The first one is done for you**

1. walk _*quietly*_

2. smiled _____

3. painted _____

4. laughed _____

5. arrived _____

6. folded _____

7. _____ run

8. _____ looked

9. burned _____

10. _____ cried

11. went _____

12. answered _____

Write five sentences using the verbs and adverbs you put together.

EXAMPLE: I will <u>walk</u> <u>quietly</u> in the library.

13. _____

14. _____

15. _____

16. _____

17. _____

Read a book and fill out the following book report. Share it with a sister, brother or friend.

Title: _____
_____
Author: _____
Illustrator: _____
Setting (where): _____
_____
Main Characters (who): _____
_____
_____
_____
Main Ideas (what): _____
_____
_____

I liked the book because: _____
_____
_____
_____
_____
_____
Tell which character in the book you would like to be and why:
_____
_____
_____
_____

Dictionary Sentences. **Rewrite the following dictionary sentences using the correct spelling.**

1. Thaŋk ū fôr thə yelʹō T shũrt and blak shərts.

   _____

2. Misʹtẽr Ralph livz ôn ə färm doun əlôŋ thə rivʹẽr.

   _____

3. I stakʹəd ôl thə kanz ôn top uv ēch uthʹẽr.

   _____

4. Wē nēd ə galʹən uv milk, sum egz, and butʹẽr, nou!

   _____

Now rewrite these two sentences using the dictionary.

1. A thousand pennies equal ten dollars, I am told.

   _____

2. Monkeys are funny, furry little animals in the zoo.

   _____

Geometry. **Explain to an adult what the following geometrical terms mean. Show what each means by drawing an example of each.**

1. Segments, lines, endpoints, and rays.

2. Intersecting lines

3. Parallel lines

4. Perimeter

• •

Adverbs tell <u>where</u>, <u>how</u>, or <u>when</u>. Tell what kind of adverb is underlined in the following sentences. Write <u>where</u>, <u>when</u>, or <u>how</u>.

1. Animals are <u>sometimes</u> called mammals. _____
2. There was a big accident on the freeway <u>yesterday</u>. _____
3. Joe <u>quickly</u> ran out to catch the bus. _____
4. We could hear the sound far <u>below</u> us. _____
5. Our campfire burned <u>brightly</u> all night. _____
6. We are going <u>there</u> next winter. _____
7. Be sure and write your letter <u>neatly</u>. _____
8. The birds will fly <u>away</u> if you scare them. _____
9. Father is going to leave <u>immediately</u>. _____
10. The baby played <u>happily</u> on the lawn. _____

Now fill in the blanks with a <u>how</u>, <u>when</u>, or <u>where</u> adverb.

1. The car was going very (how) _____.
2. Will you take April and June (where) _____ to the movie?
3. Mom will take them down (when) _____.

Add one or two syllables to the words below to make two new words. Make sure you spell the words correctly.

EXAMPLE: **low**   **pillow**   **follow**

1. law _____ _____
2. place _____ _____
3. rock _____ _____
4. tire _____ _____
5. band _____ _____
6. bat _____ _____
7. bit _____ _____
8. sent _____ _____
9. sand _____ _____
10. car _____ _____
11. ham _____ _____
12. out _____ _____

13. able _____ _____
14. age _____ _____
15. ten _____ _____
16. man _____ _____
17. cat _____ _____
18. son _____ _____
19. con _____ _____
20. be _____ _____
21. play _____ _____
22. star _____ _____
23. stand _____ _____
24. hob _____ _____

It's important to know what the following words mean, especially when you're taking a test. Circle the letter that gives the best meaning for the underlined words in the sentence.

1. Can you <u>solve</u> this problem?
   a. copy   b. answer   c. recall
2. Make an <u>estimate</u> of how many people are in the U.S.
   a. approximate guess   b. count them   c. rank them
3. Let's take a <u>survey</u> of people who like red licorice.
   a. find out   b. examine   c. select
4. Will you <u>complete</u> your test in ten minutes?
   a. support   b. utilize   c. finish
5. Do <u>sections</u> one and two on this page.
   a. groups   b. parts   c. areas
6. Post office workers <u>classify</u> mail according to locations.
   a. change   b. write   c. arrange or group
7. We were pleased with our <u>survey</u> of the house.
   a. examination   b. explain   c. understanding
8. You will have to <u>prove</u> your answers.
   a. sample   b. question   c. to show as right and true
9. Do you understand the <u>directions</u>?
   a. why   b. describe it   c. how to do
10. Spencer <u>usually</u> knows the right answers.
    a. never   b. always   c. most of the time
11. You have to <u>apply</u> yourself if you want to get good grades.
    a. work and stick to it   b. justify   c. recommend
12. Read the book and <u>summarize</u> it for the class.
    a. reread   b. express briefly   c. show how

More Geometry. **Explain and draw an example of the following geometrical terms.**

1. Congruent figures

2. Right angles

3. Triangles

4. Parallelograms

5. Polygons

Sometimes it's fun to share a story with someone else. Read a book, then call one of your friends or go visit them. Tell your friend about the book you read.

Tell who the main characters are. Tell where the story takes place. Tell the plot-main event of the story. But don't tell them how the story ends. See if you can get them to read the book.

On the rest of the page, write what happened. Did you get your friend to read the book?

_____

_____

_____

_____

_____

_____

_____

_____

_____

Day 14

Create small words from letters in the following words. Write them. You may find more than one in most words.

EXAMPLE: borrow *row*   or   *bow*   *rob*

1. pajamas _____
2. carpenter _____
3. performance_____
4. bandage _____
5. knowledge _____
6. theory _____
7. satisfaction _____
8. customer _____
9. discovery _____
10. eventually_____
11. announcement_____
12. sentence _____
13. theater _____
14. honorable_____
15. investigate _____

Sometimes things happen that cause something else to happen. This is called "cause and effect." A clue word helps to tell which is which. In the following sentences, underline the cause with a straight line (___). Underline the effect with a dotted line (_ _ _). Put a box ☐ around the clue word. The first one is done for you.

1. The tooth was broken, ☐so☐ it gave her a lot of pain.
2. The book was ripped and dirty because the dog got it.
3. Because it was so cold, Betty could ice skate for only a short while.
4. I went to bed early last night because I was so tired.
5. Since it was raining so hard, we couldn't play outside.
6. The rabbit ran fast because the fox was after it.
7. It was very foggy out, so we could not see the mountains.
8. Because we got to the camp late in the day, there was no time for hiking.
9. It was very dark in the dugout, so we turned on the flashlight.
10. Kit played basketball too long after school, therefore, he missed the bus.
11. Laura's letter was returned because she forgot to put a stamp on it.
12. Mike's suitcase broke when it fell off the car. As a result, he had to put his things in a paper bag.

Graphs, Charts, and Tables. There are many different kinds of graphs, charts, and tables. Check your newspaper regularly to find different kinds and different information that you could chart or graph daily. This is a "broken-line" graph. Complete this graph using the information given in the table.
Monday and Tuesday have been done for you.

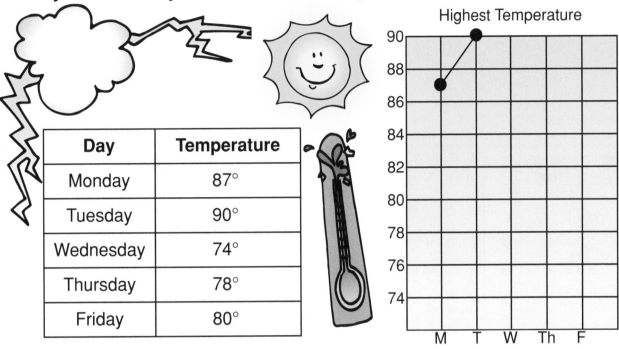

Day	Temperature
Monday	87°
Tuesday	90°
Wednesday	74°
Thursday	78°
Friday	80°

Write these sentences in the correct order. Underline the negative word in each sentence. The word that makes the sentence mean "no" or "not" is the negative word.

1. win won't contest I ever art an.

_____

2. involved does want be not He to.

_____

3. today I do have to no work more.

_____

4. nowhere play is us ball There for to.

_____

5. complains leg about never her She broken.

_____

6. ridden ever horse Jeremy a hasn't.

_____

Match the definitions below to a word in the word box. Find and circle the words in the puzzle. The first one has been done for you.

1. ABC order
2. not a vowel
3. more than one
4. names things
5. mark used for stress
6. part of a word
7. describes nouns
8. used in place of a noun
9. added to the beginning of a base word
10. just one
11. describes verbs
12. not a consonant
13. added to the end of a base word
14. shows action

Word Box

___vowel

___plural

___syllable

_1_ alphabetical

___consonant

___prefix

___adjectives

___nouns

___verb

___suffix

___pronoun

___adverbs

___accent

___singular

```
i z x a b u i o m e c f i t x z o c p r u t
u p r t v x o n l k b d f h j l i o m q s t
o o q s u i z a m j a c e g i k o n o u n s
j t s b r c i m s u f f i x b n o s r s t v
f d l v e r b i y q l i g h g a c o d f k l
b c u o x o k r l p u u i o t v e n e h i m
a a f w d z j (a l p h a b e t i c a l) i p m
p x c e g t l m a x q b c l l b c n j b o t
r u o l n p o k b a d g j t o t f t u a i i
y a d v e r b s l c f i l o p r e f i x e l
k d x f g j k l e b e h k i r b f g o e n e
m j z h i o q s r v x y z a o a c c e n t o
l e c m o n p t u l w e a l n w x y z a b c
a c d w e f h j l m n o q r o n o x y z e l
p t e a b e m o e g h i p l u r a l i m o t
s i n g u l a r f j k n i o n e a k l u p x
y v c d e a d e j m v y z i t m l o x z b a
o e b f g k n o q s w f o u l n a d g i m n
e s c h i l p r t y x b c e f h k l o r s t
```

Words to Sound, Read, and Spell

aboard	birthday	closet	data	earlier	fortunate	honor
accept	blindfold	clue	daughter	earliest	fortune	honorable
accident	boathouse	clumsier	dawn	early	forward	hoof
account	bookcase	clumsiest	debt	earthquake	foster	hospital
ache	boring	clumsy	decision	echo	foundation	hotel
across	borrow	clutch	declare	echoing	fountain	huge
actress	boulevard	coach	defense	editor	fourth	human
additional	bowl	coal	definite	education	frequent	humor
advice	breathless	coast	degree	effort	fright	iceberg
advise	bridge	coil	delayed	either	fuel	idea
affect	bridle	collect	delicate	eldest	furious	imagine
afford	brief	collection	delivery	electric	furnace	impatient
agency	brow	comfort	demand	electricity	furniture	import
agree	bruise	comfortable	dentist	enemies	future	important
agriculture	bucket	comical	describe	enemy	gable	impossible
alligator	build	commander	desert	engine	gain	increase
aloud	built	committee	deserve	enormous	gallon	index
alphabet	bulb	community	despite	enough	garage	indicate
already	burglar	companion	dessert	enthusiasm	geese	innocent
although	bury	company	detective	entrance	generation	inquire
among	bushel	concerns	determination	environment	genuine	insect
ancient	busiest	conference	determine	envy	germ	inspiring
ankle	business	confess	development	equal	glare	instance
announce-	busy	confirm	diamond	equipment	glaring	instant
ment	cabin	confusion	dictionary	escape	glorious	instead
answer	cabinet	conjunction	difference	especially	gnaw	institutions
anxious	camera	connect	different	estate	goodness	instructions
appearance	campaign	conquer	difficult	eventually	goose	intention
appreciate	canoes	constant	dignity	evidence	government	interest
approach	captain	contain	dining	exact	governor	interjection
approval	caption	continue	direct	except	graceful	international
approximately	caravan	contribution	director	exchange	graduated	interview
apron	cardboard	conversation	disagree	excitement	graph	introduction
aren't	carefully	convince	disappear	excuse	grateful	investigate
aroma	carpenter	copper	disappoint	exercise	gratitude	island
arranged	carpet	correctly	disaster	exercising	great	jelly
arrival	cartwheel	correspond	discover	existence	grief	jewelry
article	category	cottage	discovery	expect	groan	judgment
assistant	cattle	council	disease	expensive	groceries	juice
association	cedar	country	distance	experience	grocery	junior
assortment	ceiling	county	distant	explanation	grow	justice
assume	center	couple	distrust	explore	grown	kettle
attend	century	coupling	divide	factories	grown-up	kindness
attention	certain	courage	divided	factory	guarantee	kingdom
attic	certainly	cousin	division	familiar	guard	kneel
audience	chalk	cowboy	dizziest	famous	guilty	knit
auditorium	chamber	cozier	dizzy	fancy	habit	knob
author	champion	cozy	doctor	fantastic	hadn't	know
avenue	character	cradle	does	farewell	hail	knowledge
backward	charcoal	crawl	doesn't	farther	handkerchief	known
baggage	cheerful	crazy	dollar	faultless	handsome	label
balcony	chemist	cream	donkeys	favor	happiness	laid
balloon	cherish	creative	doubt	favorite	harness	language
banana	chicken	creature	downstairs	features	haunt	lantern
bathe	chief	crew	downtown	fiction	hawk	laughter
bathroom	chocolate	crossroads	doze	field	he's	lecture
battery	choice	crow	dozen	financial	headquarters	length
battle	choicest	cube	drawer	flapped	health	lettuce
beautiful	choose	cure	drew	flapping	heartily	level
beauty	chose	curious	dried	flattered	heavy	lever
bedtime	chuckled	current	dry	flavor	height	library
beet	circle	curtain	due	flock	histories	lie
behave	circus	custom	dumb	footprint	history	lied
believe	circuses	customer	dump	forecast	hobby	lightning
between	claim	dairy	eagle	forenoon	holiday	limb
bicycle	climate	dangerous	eardrum	forest	homemade	limping

Words to Sound, Read, and Spell

linen	northwest	pollution	region	shield	support	unlock
lion	notebook	porch	regular	shine	suspect	unlucky
liquid	nothing	position	reindeer	shone	suspicious	upstairs
listen	notice	possess	relate	shoulder	sweater	urge
litter	noun	possible	relative	shouldn't	sweet	urged
lonelier	oasis	postscript	relief	show	sword	urgent
loneliest	obey	potato	remarkable	shown	syllable	useless
lonely	object	potatoes	remember	sigh	synonym	usual
loosen	occur	pound	repair	sight	teach	vacant
losing	ocean	poverty	repeat	signal	teapot	vain
loss	offer	powder	replace	silence	teaspoon	valuable
lumber	office	practically	replied	simple	teenagers	vanish
machine	often	practice	reply	singular	teeth	variety
machinery	opposite	practicing	report	sleigh	telephone	various
mail	orchard	praise	reputation	slept	television	vary
male	ordinary	precious	rescue	slice	tennis	vegetable
mankind	original	prefer	resign	slight	terrible	versus
mansion	orphan	prejudice	respect	slim	terrific	victory
market	ounce	preposition	response	slippery	territory	view
marry	outlook	preserve	restore	smooth	thaw	violin
marvelous	package	president	retreat	snake	there's	vision
material	paddle	pressure	reward	soar	they've	volume
meadow	pair	price	rise	society	thief	waist
meal	pajamas	pricing	road	soldier	thigh	wait
mean	palm	principal	robin	sorrow	thirsty	walnut
meant	pane	private	rocket	south	thought	warehouse
measure	partial	privilege	route	soybean	thousand	warn
measured	particular	probably	rude	spare	thread	wasn't
measuring	pass	proceed	ruin	sparrow	throughout	waste
medal	passage	professional	safety	specific	thumb	we're
medicine	past	professor	sailor	speech	ticket	wealthy
medium	pasture	promise	saint	spell	tied	weary
mention	pattern	prompt	salad	spinach	tiger	weather
merchant	pause	prop	salary	splendid	tight	weigh
message	peace	prosperous	salute	spoon	toast	weight
method	peak	protect	satisfaction	sprinkle	toe	welcome
midst	pear	prove	satisfy	squeeze	together	weren't
mineral	peddle	provide	Saturday	standard	tomato	wheat
minus	peek	prune	sawdust	staring	tongue	where's
minute	perfect	publicity	scarce	statement	tool	whether
mirror	performance	puddle	scarcest	station	toothbrush	whirl
miserable	perhaps	pupil	scene	statue	topic	whistle
mission	petal	purpose	schedule	steal	topsoil	whistling
mistake	piano	purse	scholarship	steel	total	who's
mixture	picnic	quality	science	stew	toward	whom
model	picnicking	quart	scissors	sting	tractor	widow
modern	picture	quarter	season	stomach	traffic	wilderness
moisture	picturing	question	secret	straight	transportation	windshield
moment	piece	quiet	secretary	strain	treasure	wise
month	pigeon	quite	seldom	street	treatment	wolf
moonlight	plain	radish	selfish	stressed	tremendous	woman
most	plane	railroad	senator	stripe	trial	women
motion	planet	rather	senior	stroke	tried	wonderful
mountain	plantation	reach	sense	struggle	trouble	world
museum	platform	real	sensible	stumble	true	worm
musician	pleasant	reappear	sentencing	success	tune	worried
nation	pleasure	rearrange	separate	successes	typewriter	worry
nature	plural	recall	serious	suggest	unfold	worrying
nearby	pocket	recess	serve	suit	unhappy	worth
neat	poison	recognition	service	suitcase	uniform	wouldn't
necklace	poisonous	recommend	settlement	sunburn	union	wreck
necktie	police	record	several	sunshine	universal	wrestle
needle	policing	recover	severe	superintend-	university	wrist
neighbor	polish	recovery	shadow	ent	unknown	you've
nervous	polite	reference	sharpener	supply	unlike	yourself
newsreel	political	refrigerator	she'll	supplying	unload	yourselves

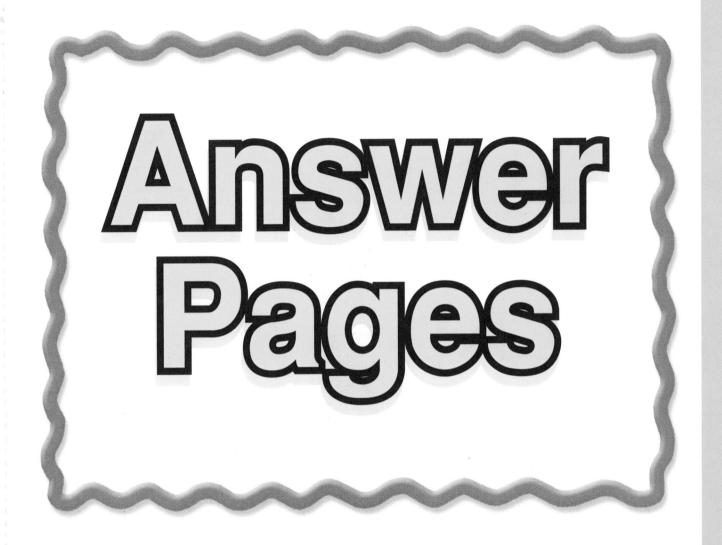

Section 1

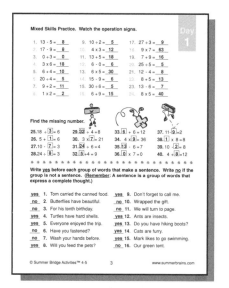

Mixed Skills Practice. Watch the operation signs.

1. 13 - 5 = 8	9. 10 ÷ 2 = 5	17. 27 ÷ 3 = 9
2. 17 - 9 = 8	10. 4 x 3 = 12	18. 9 x 7 = 63
3. 0 ÷ 3 = 0	11. 13 - 6 = 7	19. 7 x 9 = 16
4. 3 x 6 = 18	12. 6 - 0 = 6	20. 25 ÷ 5 = 5
5. 6 + 4 = 10	13. 6 x 5 = 30	21. 12 - 4 = 8
6. 20 ÷ 4 = 5	14. 15 - 9 = 6	22. 8 + 5 = 13
7. 9 ÷ 2 = 11	15. 30 ÷ 6 = 5	23. 13 - 6 = 7
8. 1 x 2 = 2	16. 6 + 9 = 15	24. 8 x 5 = 40

Find the missing number.

25. 18 ÷ 3 = 6   29. 32 ÷ 4 = 8   33. 6 ÷ 6 = 12   37. 11 - 9 = 2
26. 5 + 1 = 6   30. 3 x 7 = 21   34. 4 x 9 = 36   38. 1 x 8 = 8
27. 10 - 7 = 3   31. 24 ÷ 4 = 6   35. 13 - 6 = 7   39. 10 - 2 = 8
28. 24 - 9 = 3   32. 5 + 4 = 9   36. 0 x 7 = 0   40. 4 + 8 = 12

Write **yes** before each group of words that make a sentence. Write **no** if the group is not a sentence. (Remember: A sentence is a group of words that express a complete thought.)

yes 1. Tom carried the canned food.
no 2. Butterflies have beautiful.
no 3. For his tenth birthday.
yes 4. Turtles have hard shells.
yes 5. Everyone enjoyed the trip.
no 6. Have you fastened?
no 7. Wash your hands before.
yes 8. Will you feed the pets?
yes 9. Don't forget to call me.
no 10. Wrapped the gift.
no 11. We will turn to page.
yes 12. Ants are insects.
yes 13. Do you have hiking boots?
yes 14. Cats are furry.
yes 15. Mark likes to go swimming.
no 16. Our green tent.

© Summer Bridge Activities™ 4-5   3   www.summerbrains.com

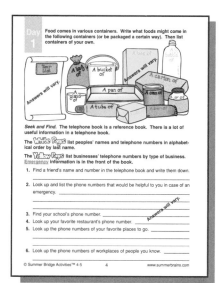

Food comes in various containers. Write what foods might come in the following containers (or be packaged a certain way). Then list containers of your own.

Answers will vary.

Seek and Find. The telephone book is a reference book. There is a lot of useful information in a telephone book.

The White Pages list peoples' names and telephone numbers in alphabetical order by last name.
The Yellow Pages list businesses' telephone numbers by type of business.
Emergency information is in the front of the book.

1. Find a friend's name and number in the telephone book and write them down.
2. Look up and list the phone numbers that would be helpful to you in case of an emergency.
3. Find your school's phone number.
4. Look up your favorite restaurant's phone number.
5. Look up the phone numbers of your favorite places to go.
6. Look up the phone numbers of workplaces of people you know.

Answers will vary.

© Summer Bridge Activities™ 4-5   4   www.summerbrains.com

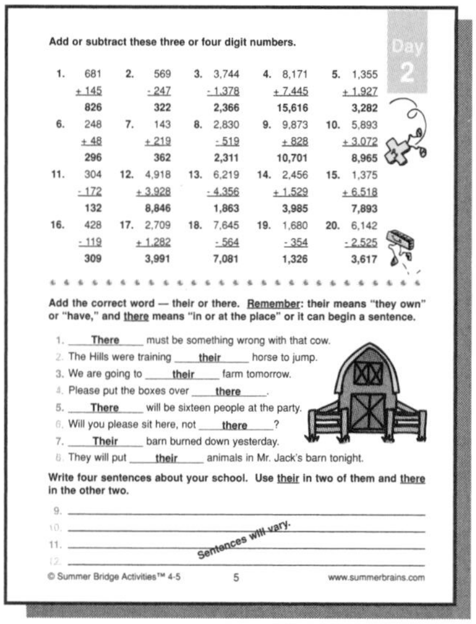

Add or subtract these three or four digit numbers.

1. 681 +145 = 826	2. 569 -247 = 322	3. 3,744 -1,378 = 2,366	4. 8,171 +7,445 = 15,616	5. 1,355 +1,927 = 3,282
6. 248 +48 = 296	7. 143 +219 = 362	8. 2,830 -519 = 2,311	9. 9,873 +828 = 10,701	10. 5,893 +3,072 = 8,965
11. 304 -172 = 132	12. 4,918 +3,928 = 8,846	13. 6,219 -4,356 = 1,863	14. 2,456 +1,529 = 3,985	15. 1,375 +6,518 = 7,893
16. 428 -119 = 309	17. 2,709 +1,282 = 3,991	18. 7,645 -564 = 7,081	19. 1,680 -354 = 1,326	20. 6,142 -2,525 = 3,617

Add the correct word — **their** or **there**. Remember: **their** means "they own" or "have," and **there** means "in or at the place" or it can begin a sentence.

1. There must be something wrong with that cow.
2. The Hills were training their horse to jump.
3. We are going to their farm tomorrow.
4. Please put the boxes over there.
5. Will you please sit here, not there?
6. There will be sixteen people at the party.
7. Their barn burned down yesterday.
8. They will put their animals in Mr. Jack's barn tonight.

Write four sentences about your school. Use **their** in two of them and **there** in the other two.

9. _____
10. _____
11. _____
12. _____

Sentences will vary.

© Summer Bridge Activities™ 4-5   5   www.summerbrains.com

Suffixes. A suffix is a syllable added to the end of a base word. Add the suffix in the middle of the suffix wheel to the end of the base word. Write the new word. Remember: You may need to double the final consonant or change a (y) to an (i) when adding a suffix.

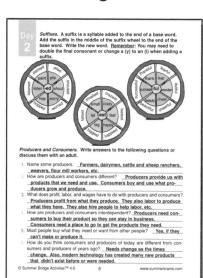

Producers and Consumers. Write answers to the following questions or discuss them with an adult.

1. Name some producers. Farmers, dairymen, cattle and sheep ranchers, weavers, flour mill workers, etc.
2. How are producers and consumers different? Producers provide us with products that we need and use. Consumers buy and use what producers grow and produce.
3. What does profit, labor, and wages have to do with producers and consumers? Producers profit from what they produce. They also labor to produce what they have. They also hire people to help labor, etc.
4. How are producers and consumers interdependent? Producers need consumers to buy their product so they can stay in business. Consumers need a place to go to get the products they need.
5. Must people buy what they need or want from other people? Yes, if they can't make or produce it.
6. How do you think consumers and producers of today are different from consumers and producers of years ago? Needs change as the times change. Also, modern technology has created many new products that didn't exist before or were needed.

© Summer Bridge Activities™ 4-5   6   www.summerbrains.com

Understanding Thousands. Write each number in standard form. The first one has been done for you.

1. 8 thousands, 3 tens, 9 ones — 8,039
2. 1 thousand, 7 tens, 5 ones — 1,075
3. 6,000 + 300 + 10 + 2 — 6,312
4. 2,000 + 900 + 80 + 9 — 2,989
5. 3 thousands, 8 hundreds, 4 tens, 1 one — 3,841
6. 6 thousands, 9 hundreds, 9 tens, 6 ones — 6,996
7. 5,000 + 700 + 3 — 5,703
8. 1,000 + 400 + 10 — 1,410
9. 7 thousands, 1 hundred, 7 ones — 7,107
10. 1 thousand, 4 hundreds, 7 tens — 1,470
11. 9,000 + 900 + 90 + 9 — 9,999
12. 7,000 + 900 + 5 — 7,905
13. 2 thousands, 9 hundreds, 6 tens, 2 ones — 2,962
14. 4 thousands, 5 tens — 4,050
15. 1,000 + 8 — 1,008
16. 3,000 + 10 + 5 — 3,015

Read the following paragraph and answer the questions.

Kangaroos are furry, hopping mammals that live only in Australia. Antelope kangaroos live on the plains in the north. Gray kangaroos live mostly in the grasslands and forests of eastern and southern Australia. Red kangaroos make their home in the deserts and dry grasslands in the central part of the country, and most wallaroos live in dry, rocky hills.

1. What is the main idea of this paragraph? Where kangaroos live in Australia
Answers may vary.
2. List some of the important details of the paragraph? Kangaroos are furry, hopping mammals. The kinds of kangaroos and where they live. (Child could write the kinds of kangaroos and where they are found.)
Answers may vary.

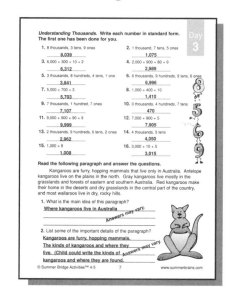

© Summer Bridge Activities™ 4-5   7   www.summerbrains.com

Products. What products might we get from the seven major regions of our country? See if you can put the correct region next to the correct products.

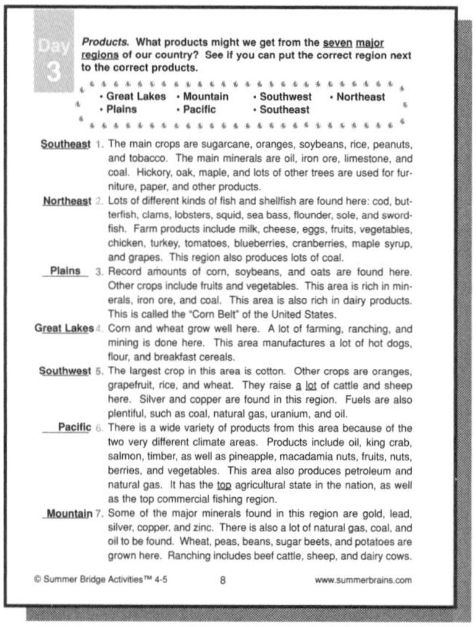

• Great Lakes   • Mountain   • Southwest   • Northeast
• Plains   • Pacific   • Southeast

Southeast 1. The main crops are sugarcane, oranges, soybeans, rice, peanuts, and tobacco. The main minerals are oil, iron ore, limestone, and coal. Hickory, oak, maple, and lots of other trees are used for furniture, paper, and other products.

Northeast 2. Lots of different kinds of fish and shellfish are found here: cod, butterfish, clams, lobsters, squid, sea bass, flounder, sole, and swordfish. Farm products include milk, cheese, eggs, fruits, vegetables, chicken, turkey, tomatoes, blueberries, cranberries, maple syrup, and grapes. This region also produces lots of coal.

Plains 3. Record amounts of corn, soybeans, and oats are found here. Other crops include fruits and vegetables. This area is rich in minerals, iron ore, and coal. This area is also rich in dairy products. This is called the "Corn Belt" of the United States.

Great Lakes 4. Corn and wheat grow well here. A lot of farming, ranching, and mining is done here. This area manufactures a lot of hot dogs, flour, and breakfast cereals.

Southwest 5. The largest crop in this area is cotton. Other crops are oranges, grapefruit, rice, and wheat. They raise a lot of cattle and sheep here. Silver and copper are found in this region. Fuels are also plentiful, such as coal, natural gas, uranium, and oil.

Pacific 6. There is a wide variety of products from this area because of the two very different climate areas. Products include oil, king crab, salmon, timber, as well as pineapple, macadamia nuts, fruits, nuts, berries, and vegetables. This area also produces petroleum and natural gas. It has the top agricultural state in the nation, as well as the top commercial fishing region.

Mountain 7. Some of the major minerals found in this region are gold, lead, silver, copper, and zinc. There is also a lot of natural gas, coal, and oil to be found. Wheat, peas, beans, sugar beets, and potatoes are grown here. Ranching includes beef cattle, sheep, and dairy cows.

© Summer Bridge Activities™ 4-5   8   www.summerbrains.com

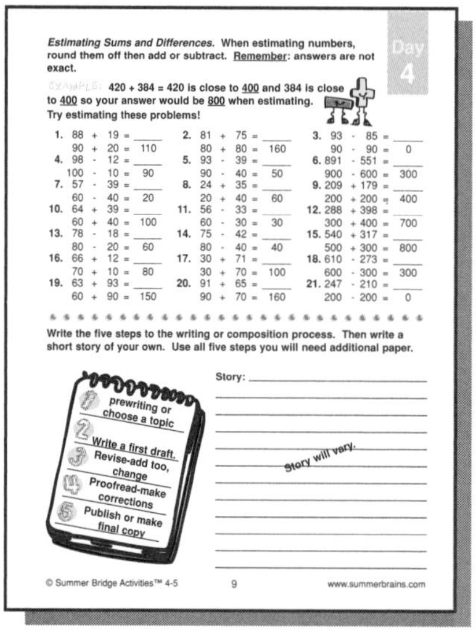

Estimating Sums and Differences. When estimating numbers, round them off then add or subtract. Remember: answers are not exact.

EXAMPLE: 420 + 384 = 420 is close to 400 and 384 is close to 400 so your answer would be 800 when estimating. Try estimating these problems!

1. 88 + 19 =	2. 81 + 75 =	3. 93 - 85 =
90 + 20 = 110	80 + 80 = 160	90 - 90 = 0
4. 98 - 12 =	5. 93 - 39 =	6. 891 - 551 =
100 - 10 = 90	90 - 40 = 50	900 - 600 = 300
7. 57 - 39 =	8. 24 + 35 =	9. 209 + 179 =
60 - 40 = 20	20 + 40 = 60	200 + 200 = 400
10. 544 + 39 =	11. 56 - 33 =	12. 288 + 398 =
60 + 40 = 100	60 - 30 = 30	300 + 400 = 700
13. 76 - 18 =	14. 75 - 42 =	15. 540 + 317 =
80 - 20 = 60	80 - 40 = 40	500 + 300 = 800
16. 66 + 12 =	17. 30 + 71 =	18. 610 - 273 =
70 + 10 = 80	30 + 70 = 100	600 - 300 = 300
19. 63 + 93 =	20. 91 + 65 =	21. 247 - 210 =
60 + 90 = 150	90 + 70 = 160	200 - 200 = 0

Write the five steps to the writing or composition process. Then write a short story of your own. Use all five steps you will need additional paper.

1. prewriting or choose a topic
2. Write a first draft.
3. Revise-add too, change
4. Proofread-make corrections
5. Publish or make final copy

Story: _____
Story will vary.

© Summer Bridge Activities™ 4-5   9   www.summerbrains.com

Prefixes. Prefixes are syllables added to the beginning of a base word. Add a prefix to these base words. The first one has been done for you.

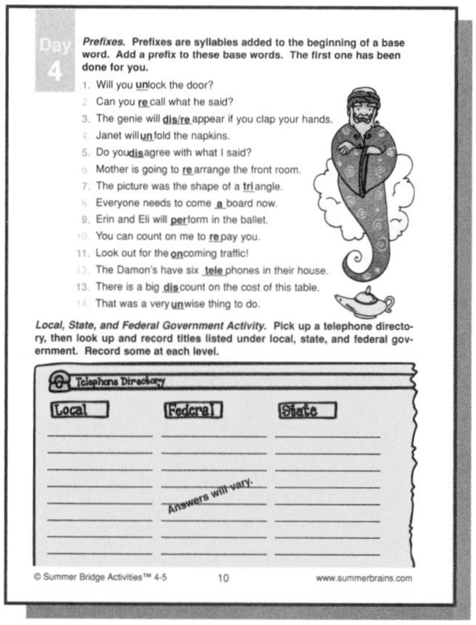

1. Will you unlock the door?
2. Can you recall what he said?
3. The genie will disappear if you clap your hands.
4. Janet will unfold the napkins.
5. Do you disagree with what I said?
6. Mother is going to rearrange the front room.
7. The picture was the shape of a triangle.
8. Everyone needs to come aboard now.
9. Erin and Eli will perform in the ballet.
10. You can count on me to repay you.
11. Look out for the oncoming traffic!
12. The Damon's have six telephones in their house.
13. There is a big discount on the cost of this table.
14. That was a very unwise thing to do.

Local, State, and Federal Government Activity. Pick up a telephone directory, then look up and record titles listed under local, state, and federal government. Record some at each level.

Telephone Directory

Local	Federal	State

Answers will vary.

© Summer Bridge Activities™ 4-5   10   www.summerbrains.com

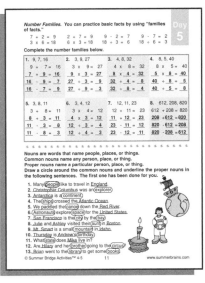

Number Families. You can practice basic facts by using "families of facts."

Day 5

7 + 2 = 9 2 + 7 = 9 9 - 2 = 7 9 - 7 = 2
3 x 6 = 18 6 x 3 = 18 18 ÷ 3 = 6 18 ÷ 6 = 3

Complete the number families below.

1. 9, 7, 16	2. 3, 9, 27	3. 4, 8, 32	4. 8, 5, 40
9 + 7 = 16	3 x 9 = 27	4 x 8 = 32	8 x 5 = 40
7 + 9 = 16	9 x 3 = 27	8 x 4 = 32	5 x 8 = 40
16 - 9 = 7	27 ÷ 3 = 9	32 ÷ 4 = 8	40 ÷ 8 = 5
16 - 7 = 9	27 ÷ 9 = 3	32 ÷ 8 = 4	40 ÷ 5 = 8
5. 3, 8, 11	6. 3, 4, 12	7. 12, 11, 23	8. 612, 208, 820
3 + 8 = 11	3 x 4 = 12	12 + 11 = 23	612 + 208 = 820
8 + 3 = 11	4 x 3 = 12	11 + 12 = 23	208 + 612 = 820
11 - 3 = 8	12 ÷ 3 = 4	23 - 11 = 12	820 - 612 = 208
11 - 8 = 3	12 ÷ 4 = 3	23 - 12 = 11	820 - 208 = 612

Nouns are words that name people, places, or things.
Common nouns name any person, place, or thing.
Proper nouns name a particular person, place, or thing.
Draw a circle around the common nouns and underline the proper nouns in the following sentences. The first one has been done for you.

1. Many (people) like to travel in England.
2. Christopher Columbus was an (explorer).
3. Antarctica is a (continent).
4. The (ships) crossed the Atlantic Ocean.
5. We paddled the (canoe) down the Red River.
6. (Astronauts) explore (space) for the United States.
7. San Francisco is the (city) by the (bay).
8. Julie and Ashley visited their (aunt) in Boston.
9. Mt. Smart is a small (mountain) in Idaho.
10. Thursday is Andrew's (birthday).
11. What (state) does Mike live in?
12. Are Hilary and her (brother) going to the (circus)?
13. Brian went to the (library) to get some (books).

© Summer Bridge Activities™ 4-5 11 www.summerbrains.com

Page 11

Day 5

Draw lines between these words and their abbreviations.

EXAMPLE:

Sunday	mag.	dozen	Fri.
magazine	pd.	Friday	tel.
quart	ex.	principal	univ.
November	Sun.	telephone	pt.
paid	oz.	volume	ave.
pages	ft.	pint	Oct.
ounce	Nov.	William	wk.
package	qt.	October	prin.
Doctor	pp.	street	st.
example	govt.	university	Wm.
government	Dr.	week	vol.
foot	pkg.	avenue	doz.

Our Government. **There are three kinds of government: local, state, and federal (or national). Each kind handles problems of different sizes. They try to solve problems that people cannot solve alone. Put the following statements on problem solving and choices in the correct sequence (1,2,3,4).**

2 Write down the possible results of each choice, whether it's good or bad.
1 List all the choices or possibilities there are in connection to the problem or situation.
4 If there is more than one person involved, or if it involves money, people take a vote.
3 Decide what is most important and which choice or choices will best solve the problem.

Now choose a problem or choice that you are facing and try to follow some or all of the steps above. This problem or choice may affect just you, or it might affect those around you.

© Summer Bridge Activities™ 4-5 12 www.summerbrains.com

Page 12

Money Sense.

Day 6

1. Cammie has 3 coins with a value of 11¢. What are the coins? 2 nickels and 1 penny
2. Janet has 6 coins with the value of 47¢. What are the coins? 1 quarter, 1 dime, 2 nickels and 2 pennies
3. Frankie has 5 coins that have the value of 17¢. What 5 coins add up to 17¢? 3 nickels and 2 pennies
4. Tenley has 7 coins. The value of the coins is 20¢. Find 7 coins with the value of 20¢. 1 dime, 1 nickel and 5 pennies
5. Jake has 4 coins. One of them is a quarter. The value of his coins is 45¢. What coins does he have? 1 quarter, 1 dime, 2 nickels
6. Gary has 6 coins with a value of 40¢. Find the 6 coins that Gary has with the value of 40¢. 2 dimes 4 nickels

Singular (One) and Plural (More Than One) Nouns. **Write the singular or plural form of the following nouns.**

EXAMPLE: bee	bees	EXAMPLE: boys	boy
1. bunny	bunnies	14. windows	window
2. cities	city	15. child	children
3. toe	toes	16. libraries	library
4. buses	bus	17. movie	movies
5. branch	branches	18. goose	geese
6. foot	feet	19. deer	deer
7. sheep	sheep	20. boxes	box
8. men	man	21. class	classes
9. face	faces	22. woman	women
10. berries	berry	23. tax	taxes
11. donkey	donkeys	24. circuses	circus
12. stitch	stitches	25. turkeys	turkey
13. oxen	ox	26. book	books

© Summer Bridge Activities™ 4-5 13 www.summerbrains.com

Page 13

Day 6

Which word referent should be used in place of the word or words in parenthesis? Write it in the blank. He, she, you, it, they, him, her, them, then, here, us, and there are all word referents.

Barbara and Denise were best friends. (Barbara and Denise) They had decided to go on a trip together this summer. With maps and brochures scattered all over Barbara's floor, (Barbara and Denise) They started looking for a place to go. One brochure was telling about an interesting place, (The brochure) It was about Yellowstone Park. "Let's go (Yellowstone) there!" cried Denise. "(Yellowstone) It would be a fun place to go. I think we should ask my brother to go with us," said Barbara. "(My brother) He could do a lot of the driving for (Barbara and Denise) us."

Tom's car was packed and ready to go the next morning. (The car) It was a new 4x4 Ranger. (Barbara, Denise, and Tom) They would have taken Barbara's car but (Barbara's) Her car had a flat tire.

After driving for two days the travelers got to Yellowstone Park. Tom shouted, "At last we are (at Yellowstone) here!" (Tom) He was tired of driving. (The trip) It turned out to be a fun trip for (Denise, Barbara, and Tom) them.

Points of Interest. **What makes the state, town, or country that you live in an interesting place? Write a campaign or advertisement to get people to visit or even live in your state, town, or country. What are the points of interest? What makes it special and different from other places?**

Answers will vary.

© Summer Bridge Activities™ 4-5 14 www.summerbrains.com

Page 14

Write the number that is 10 more than the number and then write the number that is 10 less than the number. The first one is done for you.

Day 7

1. 59	2. 496	3. 951	4. 392
69, 49	506, 486	961, 941	402, 382
5. 164	6. 703	7. 73	8. 1,946
174, 154	713, 693	83, 63	1,956, 1,936

Do the same thing as above except use 100 more than the number and 100 less than the number.

9. 150	11. 555	13. 871	15. 3,102
250, 50	655, 455	971, 771	3,202, 3,002
10. 703	12. 493	14. 1,956	16. 5,691
803, 603	593, 393	2,056, 1,856	5,791, 5,591

Write a proper noun for each of the common nouns listed below.
Remember: Proper nouns start with capital letters.

EXAMPLE: building *White House*

1. National park
2. holiday
3. dam
4. state
5. river
6. person
7. desert
8. day
9. island
10. street

Answers will vary.

Now write a common noun for the following proper nouns.

1. Golden Gate bridge
2. San Francisco city
3. Pacific ocean
4. November month
5. Canada country
6. Joseph name
7. Liberty Bell monument
8. Pete's Dragon title
9. Jupiter planet
10. Indians people

© Summer Bridge Activities™ 4-5 15 www.summerbrains.com

Page 15

Day 7

Father's Day. **Write about fathers, then draw a picture. Fathers should always.... Father should never.... If I were a father I would want to always....**

Stories will vary.

Draw your picture here!

© Summer Bridge Activities™ 4-5 16 www.summerbrains.com

Page 16

Adding Thousands. **If you have a calculator, use it to check your answers.**

Day 8

1. 2,456 + 1,527 = 3,983	2. 9,873 + 1,828 = 11,701	3. 7,125 + 2,008 = 9,133	4. 4,678 + 3,321 = 7,999
5. 18,086 + 12,302 = 30,388	6. 8,377 + 13,674 = 22,051	7. 10,308 + 23,548 = 33,856	8. 19,873 + 1,828 = 21,701
9. 626 + 8,024 + 3,643 = 12,293	10. 3,481 + 309 + 4,877 = 8,667	11. 1,465 + 388 + 3,035 = 4,888	12. 430 + 2,824 + 4,099 = 7,353

A singular (one) possessive noun is usually formed by adding -'s — animal's. A plural (two or more) possessive noun is usually formed by adding - s' — animals'. Choose a singular or plural possessive noun to fill in the blanks. Hint: look at the word after the blank to help you decide if it's singular or plural.

Word Box: birds', woman's, child's, dog's, childrens', Rabbits', cows', lady's, plumbers', Ann's

1. The child's toy is broken.
2. Rabbits' tails are fluffy.
3. My dog's leash is black.
4. After the accident the plumbers' tools were all over the road.
5. The childrens' pets are in a pet show.
6. The woman's coat is made of fur.
7. We hope that Ann's picture will win the prize.
8. The cows' mooing was loud and noisy.
9. That lady's hat blew away in the wind storm.
10. The birds' nests were high up in the trees.

© Summer Bridge Activities™ 4-5 17 www.summerbrains.com

Page 17

Day 8

Write the contractions to fill in the circles of the puzzle.

1. I would — I'd
2. is not — isn't
3. they will — they'll
4. should have — should've
5. who are — who're
6. these will — these'll
7. must not — mustn't
8. there have — there've
9. need not — needn't
10. it had — it'd
11. will not — won't
12. what has — what's
13. might have — might've
14. one is — one's

Regions of Our Country. **Our country is divided into seven regions. Great Lakes, Plains, Mountain, and Pacific are all regions named after bodies of water or important landforms. The other three major regions, Southwest, Southeast, and Northeast, are named for intermediate directions. Label the seven major regions of our United States.**

1. Pacific States
2. Mountain States
3. Plain States
4. Great Lake States
5. Northeast
6. Southeast
7. Southwest

*Something to think about. What about Hawaii and Alaska? What region or immediate direction would they belong to?
Hawaii Pacific States Alaska Pacific Region/Northwest

© Summer Bridge Activities™ 4-5 18 www.summerbrains.com

Page 18

Subtracting Thousands. **Check your answers with a calculator if you have one.**

Day 9

1. 8,425 - 3,519 = 4,906	2. 4,888 - 1,777 = 3,111	3. 4,314 - 2,532 = 1,782	4. 3,826 - 49 = 3,777
5. 9,453 - 3,168 = 6,285	6. 5,835 - 1,290 = 4,545	7. 2,182 - 396 = 1,786	8. 6,922 - 5,833 = 1,089
9. 8,000 - 5,603 = 2,397	10. 2,493 - 1,617 = 876	11. 22,318 - 17,725 = 4,593	12. 57,260 - 23,458 = 33,802

Write the singular and plural possessive forms of the following nouns. The first one is done for you.

Singular	Possessive	Plural	Possessive
boy	*boy's*	boys	*boys'*
key	key's	keys	keys'
bird	bird's	birds	birds'
mouse	mouse's	mice	mice's
puppy	puppy's	puppies	puppies'
woman	woman's	women	women's
class	class's	classes	classes'
rollerblade	rollerblade's	rollerblades	rollerblades'
flag	flag's	flags	flags'
computer	computer's	computers	computers'

© Summer Bridge Activities™ 4-5 19 www.summerbrains.com

Page 19

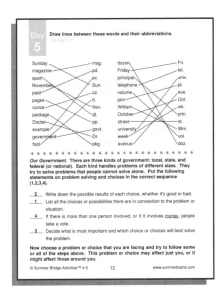

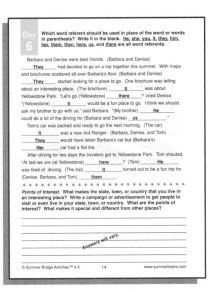

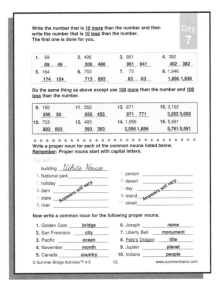

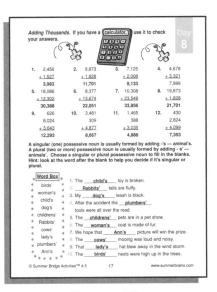

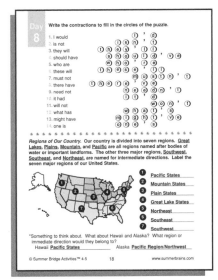

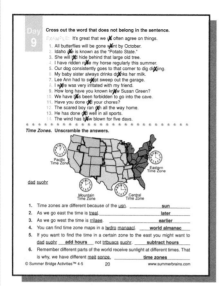

Page 20

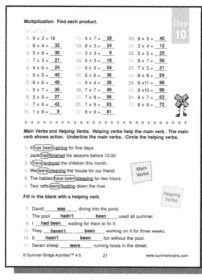

Page 21

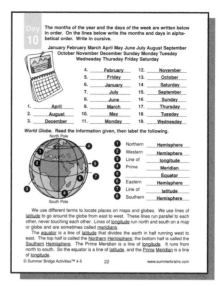

Page 22

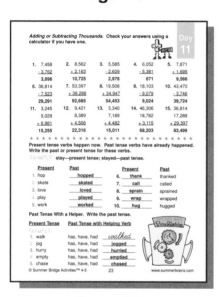

Page 23

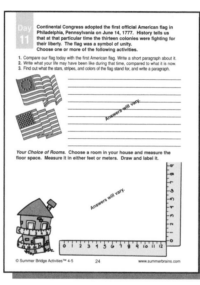

Page 24

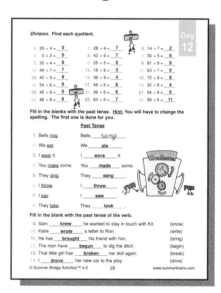

Page 25

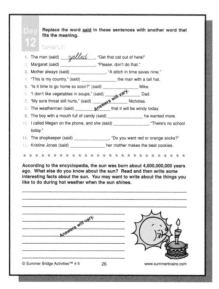

Page 26

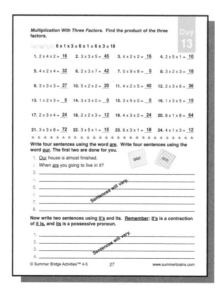

Page 27

Page 28

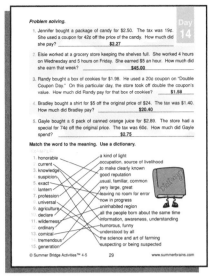

Page 29

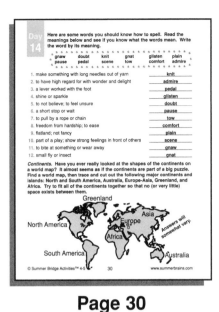

Page 30

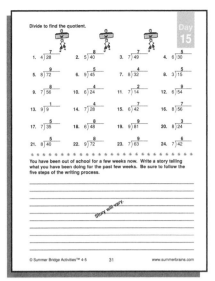

Page 31

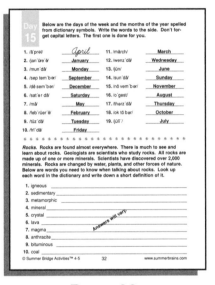

Page 32

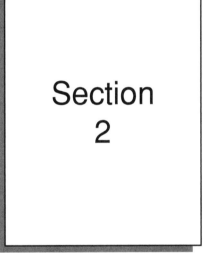

Section 2

Page 37

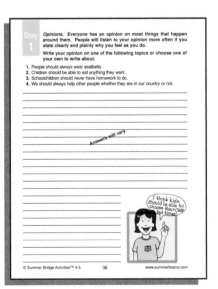

Page 38

Find the product by multiplying.

Page 39

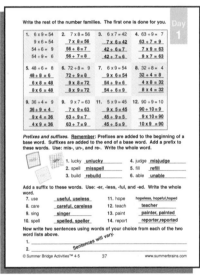

Page 40

Page 41

Complete the tables.

1. There are 5 pennies in a nickel.

pennies	5	10	15	20	25	30
nickels	1	2	3	4	5	6

2. There are 10 dimes in a dollar.

dimes	10	20	30	40	50	60
dollars	1	2	3	4	5	6

3. There are 6 cans of pop in each carton.

cans	6	12	18	24	30	36
cartons	1	2	3	4	5	6

4. You can get 6 swimming lessons for $20.

lessons	6	12	18	24	30	36
money	$20	$40	$60	$80	$100	$120

When you write something, your reader should be able to understand clearly what you are trying to say. Read the sentences below and change the underlined word to a more descriptive or exact word.

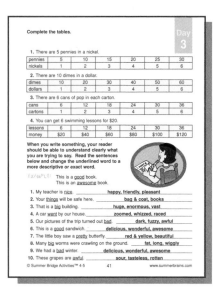

EXAMPLE: This is a good book. This is an awesome book.

1. My teacher is nice. **happy, friendly, pleasant**
2. Your things will be safe here. **bag & coat, books**
3. That is a big building. **huge, enormous, vast**
4. A car went by our house. **zoomed, whizzed, raced**
5. Our pictures of the trip turned out bad. **dark, fuzzy, awful**
6. This is a good sandwich. **delicious, wonderful, awesome**
7. The little boy saw a pretty butterfly. **red & yellow, beautiful**
8. Many big worms were crawling on the ground. **fat, long, wiggly**
9. We had a bad winter. **delicious, wonderful, awesome**
10. These grapes are awful. **sour, tasteless, rotten**

Page 42

Most words spelled backwards don't mean anything, but some do. Here are clues for some words that become different words when they are written backwards. The first one is done for you.

1. Spell a word backwards for something you cook in and you will have a word that means siesta. *pan* & *nap*
2. Spell a word backwards for a name and you will have something you turn on to get water. **pat** & **tap**
3. Spell a word backwards for something you catch a fish in and you will have a number. **net** & **ten**
4. Spell a word backwards for something to carry things in and you will get a word that tells what you like to do with your friends. **bag** & **gab**
5. Spell a word backwards for something a train needs and you will get a word for someone who is not honest. **rail** & **liar**
6. Spell a word backwards for victory and you will have a word that means "at once." **won** & **now**
7. Spell a word backwards for something to catch a mouse in and you will get a word that means something less than whole. **trap** & **part**
8. Spell a word backwards for a tool that cuts wood and you will get a word that is a verb. **saw** & **was**
9. Spell a word backwards for a flying mammal and you will get a word that means "a bill or check." **bat** & **tab**
10. Spell a word backwards for the end of your pen and you will have a word that means a hole in the ground. **tip** & **pit**
11. Spell a word backwards that means something you bathe in and you will have a word that means "other than." **tub** & **but**
12. Spell a word backwards for "an instrument used in doing work" and you will get a word that means "things taken in a robbery." **tool** & **loot**
13. Spell a word backwards for something that means "to have life" and you will get a word that means wicked. **live** & **evil**
14. Spell a word backwards for a word that means "a girl" and you will have a word that means to "fall behind." **gal** & **lag**

Page 43

Measuring in centimeters. Your little finger is about 1 centimeter wide. If you don't have a centimeter tape, use a string and this centimeter ruler to measure the following activities.

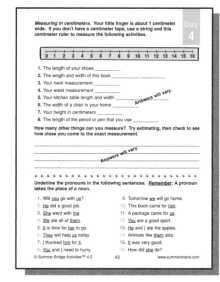

1. The length of your shoes ___
2. The length and width of this book ___
3. Your neck measurement ___
4. Your waist measurement ___
5. Your kitchen table length and width ___ *Answers will vary.*
6. The width of a chair in your home ___
7. Your height in centimeters ___
8. The length of the pencil or pen that you use ___

How many other things can you measure? Try estimating, then check to see how close you come to the exact measurement.

___ *Answers will vary.*

Underline the pronouns in the following sentences. **Remember:** A pronoun takes the place of a noun.

1. Will you go with us?
2. He did a good job.
3. She went with me.
4. We are all of them.
5. It is time for her to go.
6. They will help us today.
7. I thanked him for it.
8. You and I need to hurry.
9. Tomorrow we will go home.
10. This book came for him.
11. A package came for us.
12. You are a good sport.
13. He and I ate the apples.
14. Animals like them also.
15. It was very good.
16. How did she do?

Page 44

The Fourth of July is our nation's birthday. Another name for it is spelled out in the boxes of the puzzle. Finish the puzzle by writing the appropriate words from the word box. You will not use all of the words.

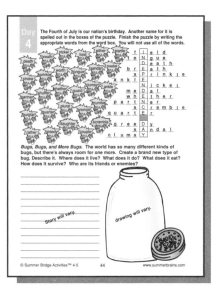

f l e d g e
N g u e
D e a t h
b r E a t h
S p r i n k l e
a n k l E
N i c k e l
m e d a l
w h E t h e r
s c r a m b l e
p a r t N e r
q u a r t e r
g r e e D y
S a n d a l
c l u m s Y

Bugs, Bugs, and More Bugs. The world has so many different kinds of bugs, but there's always room for one more. Create a brand new type of bug. Describe it. Where does it live? What does it do? What does it eat? How does it survive? Who are its friends or enemies?

Story will vary.   *drawing will vary.*

Page 45

Multiplying with tens and hundreds is fast and fun.

1. 4 x 10 = **40**
2. 600 x 6 = **3600**
3. 7 x 800 = **5,600**
4. 30 x 8 = **240**
5. 5 x 20 = **100**
6. 800 x 5 = **4,000**
7. 8 x 90 = **720**
8. 50 x 6 = **300**
9. 600 x 5 = **3,000**
10. 4 x 100 = **400**
11. 7 x 80 = **560**
12. 7 x 500 = **3,500**
13. 900 x 7 = **6,300**
14. 600 x 4 = **2,400**
15. 900 x 4 = **3,600**
16. 8 x 900 = **7,200**
17. 800 x 2 = **1,600**
18. 7 x 900 = **6,300**
19. 3 x 10 = **30**
20. 700 x 6 = **4,200**
21. 3 x 800 = **2,400**
22. 7 x 40 = **280**
23. 9 x 10 = **90**
24. 100 x 10 = **1,000**
25. 4 x 60 = **240**
26. 80 x 2 = **160**
27. 500 x 4 = **2,000**
28. 7 x 700 = **4900**
29. 30 x 8 = **240**
30. 800 x 6 = **4,800**
31. 9 x 500 = **4500**
32. 9 x 300 = **2700**
33. 300 x 5 = **1,500**

Pronouns, such as I, you, he, she, it, we, and they, can be the subject of a sentence. Read these sentences. The subject is underlined. Rewrite the sentences and use a subject pronoun in place of the underlined subject. Write in cursive.

1. Jim and I went fishing with our dad.
   We went fishing with our dad.
2. The weather was sunny and warm.
   It was sunny and warm.
3. Ann and Sue can help us with the bait.
   They can help us with the bait.
4. Mr. Jack broke his leg.
   He broke his leg.
5. Kathy is going to New York on a vacation.
   She is going to New York on a vacation.
6. Ryan will paint the scenery.
   He will paint the scenery.

Page 46

Categorize these words under one of the headings. **Hint:** There can be eight words under each heading. **Remember:** Categorizing words means to put them in groups that have something in common. One row of examples is given.

interstate	add	region	colony	oxygen	solid
bacteria	city	stop		column	inch
debate	larva	yield	basin	hexagon	canal
environment	equal	fossil	caution		intersection
measure	insect	bay		map	estimate
numerator	freedom	society	elevation	freeway	railroad
patriot	habitat	civilization	mineral	detour	quotient

Math Words	Geography Words	Transportation Words	Science Words	Social Studies Words
add	region	interstate	bacteria	colony
hexagon	hemisphere	caution	larva	debate
measure	bay	detour	insect	freedom
inch	map	intersection	solid	candidate
equal	basin	stop	oxygen	patriot
numerator	canal	speed	habitat	city
column	environment	yield	fossil	society
estimate	elevation	freeway	mineral	civilization

What About These Animals in Our Country. Buffalo, condors, and grizzly bears have all but disappeared from our country. The symbol of our country, the bald eagle, is very rare in most states. Bald eagles and bears live in mountainous regions. Prairie dogs and antelope live in the plain regions. Alligators live in marshy areas. Rattlesnakes live in the desert. Wild turkeys can be found in wilderness areas. These are all animals found in our country. There are also many others. Choose one of the following to do on a separate piece of paper.

1. Choose and draw a picture of an animal from our country. Place it in the correct habitat. Color it accurately. What other interesting animals do you think might belong in this area? Draw them. What other important information does your picture show?
2. If you choose not to draw a picture about an animal, write a paragraph about one. Use the same type of information that the picture would portray.

What animal(s) did you choose? **Answers will vary.**

Page 47

Addition and multiplication are related. Answer the addition problems and then write the related multiplication problem.

EXAMPLE: 10 + 10 + 10 + 10 + 10 = 50; 5 x 10 = 50

1. 20 + 20 + 20 = **60**   3 x 20 = 60
2. 9 + 9 + 9 + 9 + 9 + 9 = **54**   6 x 9 = 54
3. 100 + 100 + 100 + 100 = **400**   4 x 100 = 400
4. 8 + 8 + 8 + 8 + 8 + 8 + 8 + 8 = **64**   8 x 8 = 64
5. 12 + 12 + 12 + 12 = **48**   4 x 12 = 48
6. 75 + 75 + 75 = **225**   3 x 75 = 225
7. 35 + 35 + 35 + 35 + 35 + 35 = **210**   6 x 35 = 210
8. 51 + 51 + 51 + 51 + 51 = **255**   5 x 51 = 255

Use pronouns me, her, him, it, us, you, and them after action verbs. Use I and me after the other nouns or pronouns. Circle the correct pronoun in each sentence.

1. Lily and (I, me) like to visit museums.
2. (They, Them) buy very juicy oranges.
3. He helped her and (I, me).
4. (We, Us) tried not to fall as much this time.
5. Miss Green gave a shovel and bucket to (he, him).
6. (I, Me) wanted a new horse for Christmas.
7. Rick asked (she, her) to come with us.
8. Jason went with (they, them) to the mountain.
9. Mother asked (I, me) to fix the dinner.
10. Carla got some forks for (we, us).
11. Please, teach that trick to Lisa and (I, me).
12. She and (I, me) swam all day.

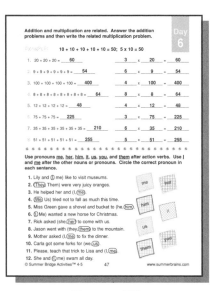

me   him   it   us   you   them

Page 48

Study this table about trees, and use it to answer the questions below. Can you identify the trees around you?

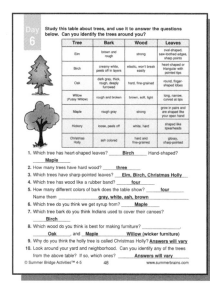

Tree	Bark	Wood	Leaves
Elm	brown and rough	strong	oval-shaped, saw-toothed edges, sharp points
Birch	creamy white, peels off in layers	elastic, won't break easily	heart-shaped or triangular with pointed tips
Oak	dark gray, thick, rough, deeply furrowed	hard, fine-grained	round, finger-shaped lobes
Willow (Pussy Willow)	rough and broken	brown, soft, light	long, narrow, curved at tips
Maple	rough gray	strong	grow in pairs and are shaped like your open hand
Hickory	loose, peels off	white, hard	shaped like spearheads
Christmas Holly	ash colored	hard and fine-grained	glossy, sharp-pointed

1. Which tree has heart-shaped leaves? **Birch** Hand-shaped? **Maple**
2. How many trees have hard wood? **three**
3. Which trees have sharp-pointed leaves? **Elm, Birch, Christmas Holly**
4. Which tree has wood like a rubber band? **four**
5. How many different colors of bark does the table show? **four**
   Name them **gray, white, ash, brown**
6. Which tree do you think we get syrup from? **Maple**
7. Which tree bark do you think Indians used to cover their canoes? **Birch**
8. Which wood do you think is best for making furniture? **Oak**, and **Maple** **Willow** (wicker furniture)
9. Why do you think the holly tree is called Christmas Holly? **Answers will vary**
10. Look around your yard and neighborhood. Can you identify any of the trees from the above table? If so, which ones? **Answers will vary**

Page 49

Complete this multiplication table.

x	10	20	30	40	50	60	70	80	90
1	10	20	30	40	50	60	70	80	90
2	20	40	60	80	100	120	140	160	180
3	30	60	90	120	150	180	210	240	270
4	40	80	120	160	200	240	280	320	360
5	50	100	150	200	250	300	350	400	450
6	60	120	180	240	300	360	420	480	540
7	70	140	210	280	350	420	490	560	630
8	80	160	240	320	400	480	560	640	720
9	90	180	270	360	450	540	630	720	810

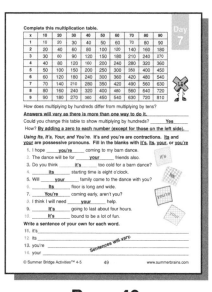

How does multiplying by hundreds differ from multiplying by tens? **Answers will vary as there is more than one way to do it.**
Could you change this table to show multiplying by hundreds? **Yes**
How? **By adding a zero to each number (except for those on the left side).**

Using Its, It's, Your, and You're. It's and you're are contractions. Its and your are possessive pronouns. Fill in the blanks with it's, its, your, or you're.

1. I hope **you're** coming to my barn dance.
2. The dance will be for **your** friends also.
3. Do you think **it's** too cold for a barn dance?
4. **Its** starting time is eight o'clock.
5. Will **your** family come to the dance with you?
6. **Its** floor is long and wide.
7. **You're** coming early, aren't you?
8. I think I will need **your** help.
9. **It's** going to last about four hours.
10. **It's** bound to be a lot of fun.

Write a sentence of your own for each word.
11. it's
12. its
13. you're
14. your
Sentences will vary.

Page 41   **Page 42**   **Page 43**
Page 44   **Page 45**   **Page 46**
Page 47   **Page 48**   **Page 49**

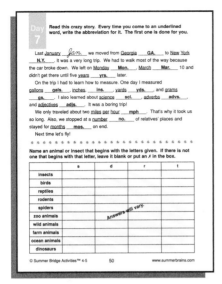

Page 50

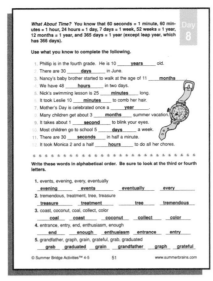

Page 51

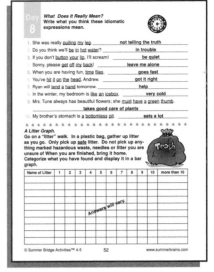

Page 52

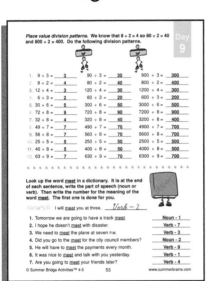

Page 53

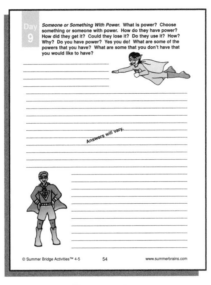

Page 54

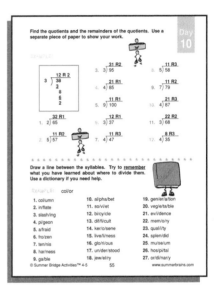

Page 55

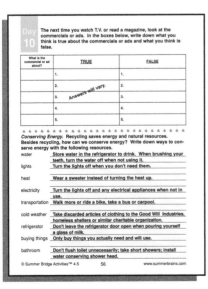

Page 56

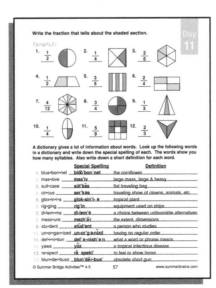

Page 57

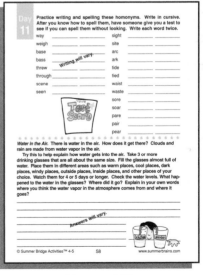

Page 58

Page 50 (Day 7): Read this crazy story. Every time you come to an underlined word, write the abbreviation for it. The first one is done for you.

Last January *Jan.* we moved from Georgia **GA.** to New York **N.Y.** It was a very long trip. We had to walk most of the way because the car broke down. We left on Monday **Mon.**, March **Mar.** 10 and didn't get there until five years **yrs.** later.

On the trip I had to learn how to measure. One day I measured gallons **gals.**, inches **ins.**, yards **yds.**, and grams **gs.**. I also learned about science **sci.**, adverbs **advs.**, and adjectives **adjs.**. It was a boring trip!

We only traveled about two miles per hour **mph**. That's why it took us so long. Also, we stopped at a number **no.** of relatives' places and stayed for months **mos.** on end.

Next time let's fly!

Name an animal or insect that begins with the letters given. If there is not one that begins with that letter, leave it blank or put an ✗ in the box.

	s	d	r	t
insects				
birds				
reptiles				
rodents				
spiders				
zoo animals				
wild animals				
farm animals				
ocean animals				
dinosaurs				

Answers will vary.

© Summer Bridge Activities™ 4-5   50   www.summerbrains.com

Page 51 (Day 8): **What About Time?** You know that 60 seconds = 1 minute, 60 minutes = 1 hour, 24 hours = 1 day, 7 days = 1 week, 52 weeks = 1 year, 12 months = 1 year, and 365 days = 1 year (except leap year, which has 366 days).

Use what you know to complete the following.

1. Phillip is in the fourth grade. He is 10 **years** old.
2. There are 30 **days** in June.
3. Nancy's baby brother started to walk at the age of 11 **months**.
4. We have 48 **hours** in two days.
5. Nick's swimming lesson is 25 **minutes** long.
6. It took Leslie 10 **minutes** to comb her hair.
7. Mother's Day is celebrated once a **year**.
8. Many children get about 3 **months** summer vacation.
9. It takes about 1 **second** to blink your eyes.
10. Most children go to school 5 **days** a week.
11. There are 30 **seconds** in half a minute.
12. It took Monica 2 and a half **hours** to do all her chores.

Write these words in alphabetical order. Be sure to look at the third or fourth letters.

1. events, evening, every, eventually
   evening   **events**   **eventually**   **every**
2. tremendous, treatment, tree, treasure
   treasure   **treatment**   **tree**   **tremendous**
3. coast, coconut, coal, collect, color
   coal   **coast**   **coconut**   **collect**   **color**
4. entrance, entry, end, enthusiasm, enough
   end   **enough**   **enthusiasm**   **entrance**   **entry**
5. grandfather, graph, grain, grateful, grab, graduated
   grab   **graduated**   **grain**   **grandfather**   **graph**   **grateful**

© Summer Bridge Activities™ 4-5   51   www.summerbrains.com

Page 52 (Day 8): **What Does It Really Mean?** Write what you think these idiomatic expressions mean.

1. She was really pulling my leg. **not telling the truth**
2. Do you think we'll be in hot water? **in trouble**
3. If you don't button your lip, I'll scream! **be quiet**
4. Sonny, please get off my back! **leave me alone**
5. When you are having fun, time flies. **goes fast**
6. You've hit it on the head, Andrew. **got it right**
7. Ryan will lend a hand tomorrow. **help**
8. In the winter, my bedroom is like an icebox. **very cold**
9. Mrs. Tune always has beautiful flowers; she must have a green thumb. **takes good care of plants**
10. My brother's stomach is a bottomless pit. **eats a lot**

A Litter Graph. Go on a "litter" walk. In a plastic bag, gather up litter as you go. Only pick up safe litter. Do not pick up anything marked hazardous waste, needles or litter you are unsure of. When you are finished, bring it home. Categorize what you have found and display it in a bar graph.

Name of Litter	1	2	3	4	5	6	7	8	9	10	more than 10

Answers will vary.

© Summer Bridge Activities™ 4-5   52   www.summerbrains.com

Page 53 (Day 9): *Place value division patterns.* We know that 8 ÷ 2 = 4 so 80 ÷ 2 = 40 and 800 ÷ 2 = 400. Do the following division patterns.

1. 9 ÷ 3 = **3**   90 ÷ 3 = **30**   900 ÷ 3 = **300**
2. 8 ÷ 2 = **4**   80 ÷ 2 = **40**   800 ÷ 2 = **400**
3. 12 ÷ 4 = **3**   120 ÷ 4 = **30**   1200 ÷ 4 = **300**
4. 6 ÷ 3 = **2**   60 ÷ 3 = **20**   600 ÷ 3 = **200**
5. 30 ÷ 6 = **5**   300 ÷ 6 = **50**   3000 ÷ 6 = **500**
6. 72 ÷ 8 = **9**   720 ÷ 8 = **90**   7200 ÷ 8 = **900**
7. 32 ÷ 8 = **4**   320 ÷ 8 = **40**   3200 ÷ 8 = **400**
8. 49 ÷ 7 = **7**   490 ÷ 7 = **70**   4900 ÷ 7 = **700**
9. 56 ÷ 8 = **7**   560 ÷ 8 = **70**   5600 ÷ 8 = **700**
10. 25 ÷ 5 = **5**   250 ÷ 5 = **50**   2500 ÷ 5 = **500**
11. 40 ÷ 8 = **5**   400 ÷ 8 = **50**   4000 ÷ 8 = **500**
12. 63 ÷ 9 = **7**   630 ÷ 9 = **70**   6300 ÷ 9 = **700**

Look up the word meet in a dictionary. It is at the end of each sentence. First, write the part of speech (noun or verb). Then write the number for the meaning of the word meet. The first one is done for you.

EXAMPLE: I will meet you at three. *Verb - 2*

1. Tomorrow we are going to have a track meet.
2. I hope he doesn't meet with disaster. **Verb - 7**
3. We need to meet the plane at seven P.M. **Verb - 3**
4. Did you go to the meet for the city council members? **Noun - 2**
5. He will have to meet the payments every month. **Verb - 9**
6. It was nice to meet and talk with you yesterday. **Verb - 1**
7. Are you going to meet your friends later? **Verb - 4**

(answer line 1: **Noun - 1**)

© Summer Bridge Activities™ 4-5   53   www.summerbrains.com

Page 54 (Day 9): **Someone or Something With Power.** What is power? Choose something or someone with power. How do they have power? How did they get it? Could they lose it? Do they use it? How? Why? Do you have power? Yes you do! What are some of the powers that you have? What are some that you don't have that you would like to have?

Answers will vary.

© Summer Bridge Activities™ 4-5   54   www.summerbrains.com

Page 55 (Day 10): Find the quotients and the remainders of the quotients. Use a separate piece of paper to show your work.

EXAMPLE:
3) 38 = 12 R 2

1. 2) 65 = **32 R1**
2. 5) 57 = **11 R2**
3. 3) 95 = **31 R2**
4. 4) 85 = **21 R1**
5. 3) 37 = **12 R1**
6. 4) 47 = **11 R3**
7. 9) 100 = **11 R1**
8. 5) 58 = **11 R3**
9. 7) 79 = **11 R2**
10. 4) 87 = **21 R3**
11. 3) 68 = **22 R2**
12. 4) 35 = **8 R3**

Draw a line between the syllables. Try to remember what you have learned about where to divide them. Use a dictionary if you need help.

EXAMPLE: col/or

1. column
2. in/flate
3. slash/ing
4. pi/geon
5. a/fraid
6. fro/zen
7. ten/nis
8. har/ness
9. ga/ble
10. al/pha/bet
11. so/vi/et
12. bi/cy/cle
13. dif/fi/cult
14. ker/o/sene
15. live/li/ness
16. glo/ri/ous
17. un/der/stood
18. jew/el/ry
19. gen/er/a/tion
20. veg/e/ta/ble
21. ev/i/dence
22. mem/o/ry
23. qual/i/ty
24. splen/did
25. mu/se/um
26. hos/pi/tal
27. or/di/nar/y

© Summer Bridge Activities™ 4-5   55   www.summerbrains.com

Page 56 (Day 10): The next time you watch T.V. or read a magazine, look at the commercials or ads. In the boxes below, write down what you think is true about the commercials or ads and what you think is false.

What is the commercial or ad about?	TRUE	FALSE
1.	1.	1.
2.	2.	2.
3.	3.	3.
4.	4.	4.
5.	5.	5.

Answers will vary.

Conserving Energy. Recycling saves energy and natural resources. Besides recycling, how can we conserve energy? Write down ways to conserve energy with the following resources.

water — **Store water in the refrigerator to drink. When brushing your teeth, turn the water off when not using it.**

lights — **Turn the lights off when you don't need them.**

heat — **Wear a sweater instead of turning the heat up.**

electricity — **Turn the lights off and any electrical appliances when not in use.**

transportation — **Walk more or ride a bike, take a bus or carpool.**

cold weather — **Take discarded articles of clothing to the Good Will Industries, homeless shelters or similar charitable organization.**

refrigerator — **Don't leave the refrigerator door open when pouring yourself a glass of milk.**

buying things — **Only buy things you actually need and will use.**

bathroom — **Don't flush toilet unnecessarily; take short showers; install water conserving shower head.**

© Summer Bridge Activities™ 4-5   56   www.summerbrains.com

Page 57 (Day 11): Write the fraction that tells about the shaded section.

EXAMPLE: 1. $\frac{1}{2}$ 2. $\frac{1}{4}$ 3. $\frac{2}{6}$

4. $\frac{1}{2}$ 5. $\frac{3}{5}$ 6. $\frac{2}{4}$

7. $\frac{1}{12}$ 8. $\frac{3}{4}$ 9. $\frac{1}{3}$

10. $\frac{1}{4}$ 11. $\frac{5}{9}$ 12. $\frac{2}{3}$

A dictionary gives a lot of information about words. Look up the following words in a dictionary and write down the special spelling of each. The words show you how many syllables. Also write down a short definition for each word.

		Special Spelling	Definition
1.	blue•bon•net	**bloo'bon'net**	the cornflower
2.	mas•sive	**mas'iv**	large mass, large & heavy
3.	suit•case	**sut'kas**	flat traveling bag
4.	cir•cus	**ser'kes**	traveling show of clowns, animals, etc.
5.	glox•in•ia	**glok-sin'i- e**	tropical plant
6.	rig•ging	**rig'in**	equipment used on ships
7.	di•lem•ma	**di-lem'e**	a choice between unfavorable alternatives
8.	meas•ure	**mezh'er**	the extent, dimensions
9.	stu•dent	**stud'ent**	a person who studies
10.	un•or•gan•ized	**un-or'g e-nizd**	having no regular order
11.	def•i•ni•tion	**def'e-nish'e n**	what a word or phrase means
12.	yaws	**yoz**	a tropical infectious disease
13.	re•spect	**re spekt'**	to feel or show honor
14.	blun•der•buss	**blun'der-bus'**	obsolete short gun

© Summer Bridge Activities™ 4-5   57   www.summerbrains.com

Page 58 (Day 11): Practice writing and spelling these homonyms. Write in cursive. After you know how to spell them, have someone give you a test to see if you can spell them without looking. Write each word twice.

way   sight
weigh   site
base   arc
bass   ark
threw   tide
through   tied
scene   waist
seen   waste
  sore
  soar
  pare
  pair
  pear

Writing will vary.

Water in the Air. There is water in the air. How does it get there? Clouds and rain are made from water vapor in the air.

Try this to help explain how water gets into the air. Take 3 or more drinking glasses that are all about the same size. Fill the glasses almost full of water. Place them in different places such as warm places, cool places, dark places, windy places, outside places, inside places, and other places of your choice. Watch them for 4 or 5 days or longer. Check the water levels. What happened to the water in the glasses? Where did it go? Explain in your own words where you think the water vapor in the atmosphere comes from and where it goes?

Answers will vary.

© Summer Bridge Activities™ 4-5   58   www.summerbrains.com

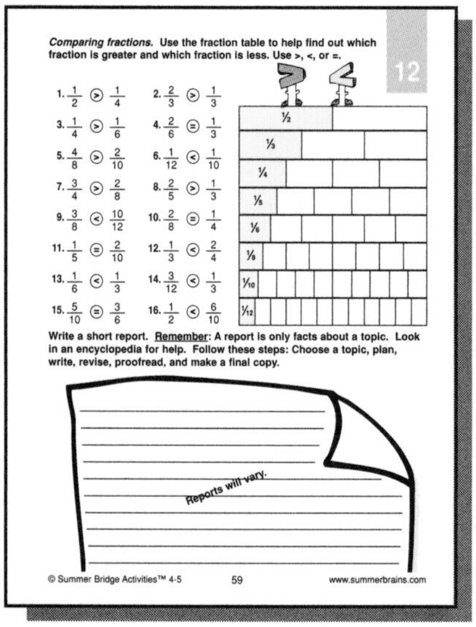

Comparing fractions. Use the fraction table to help find out which fraction is greater and which fraction is less. Use >, <, or =.

1. $\frac{1}{2} > \frac{1}{4}$ 2. $\frac{2}{3} > \frac{1}{3}$
3. $\frac{1}{4} > \frac{1}{6}$ 4. $\frac{2}{6} = \frac{1}{3}$
5. $\frac{4}{8} > \frac{2}{10}$ 6. $\frac{1}{12} < \frac{1}{10}$
7. $\frac{3}{4} > \frac{2}{8}$ 8. $\frac{2}{5} > \frac{1}{3}$
9. $\frac{3}{8} < \frac{10}{12}$ 10. $\frac{2}{8} = \frac{1}{4}$
11. $\frac{1}{5} = \frac{2}{10}$ 12. $\frac{1}{3} < \frac{2}{4}$
13. $\frac{1}{6} < \frac{1}{3}$ 14. $\frac{3}{12} < \frac{1}{3}$
15. $\frac{5}{10} < \frac{3}{6}$ 16. $\frac{1}{2} < \frac{6}{10}$

Write a short report. Remember: A report is only facts about a topic. Look in an encyclopedia for help. Follow these steps: Choose a topic, plan, write, revise, proofread, and make a final copy.

Reports will vary.

© Summer Bridge Activities™ 4-5 59 www.summerbrains.com

Page 59

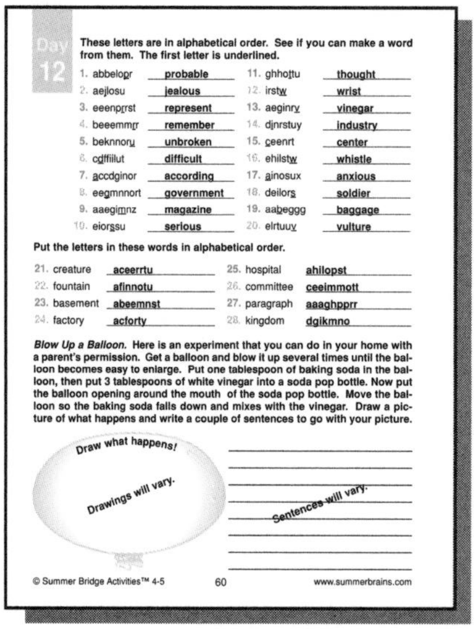

These letters are in alphabetical order. See if you can make a word from them. The first letter is underlined.

1. abbelopr probable
2. aejlosu jealous
3. eeenprrst represent
4. beeemmr remember
5. beknnoru unbroken
6. cdffilut difficult
7. accdginor according
8. eegmnnort government
9. aaegimnz magazine
10. eiorssu serious
11. ghhottu thought
12. irstw wrist
13. aeginry vinegar
14. dinrstuy industry
15. ceenrt center
16. ehilstw whistle
17. ainosux anxious
18. deilors soldier
19. aabeggg baggage
20. elrtuuv vulture

Put the letters in these words in alphabetical order.

21. creature aceerrtu
22. fountain afinnotu
23. basement abeemnst
24. factory acforty
25. hospital ahilopst
26. committee ceeimmott
27. paragraph aaaghpprr
28. kingdom dgikmno

Blow Up a Balloon. Here is an experiment that you can do in your home with a parent's permission. Get a balloon and blow it up several times until the balloon becomes easy to enlarge. Put one tablespoon of baking soda in the balloon, then put 3 tablespoons of white vinegar into a soda pop bottle. Now put the balloon opening around the mouth of the soda pop bottle. Move the balloon so the baking soda falls down and mixes with the vinegar. Draw a picture of what happens and write a couple of sentences to go with your picture.

Draw what happens! Drawings will vary. Sentences will vary.

© Summer Bridge Activities™ 4-5 60 www.summerbrains.com

Page 60

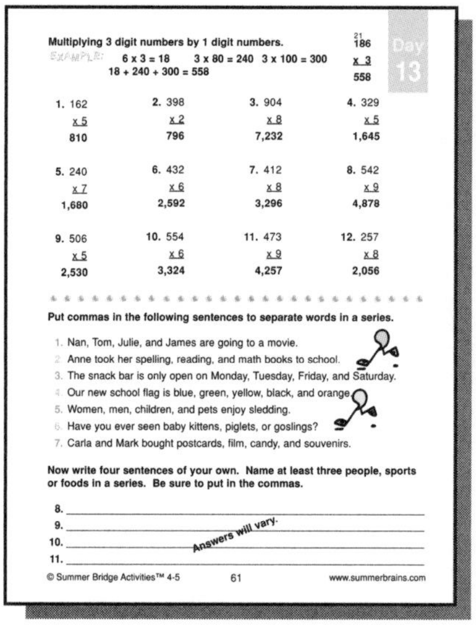

Multiplying 3 digit numbers by 1 digit numbers.

EXAMPLE: 6 x 3 = 18 3 x 80 = 240 3 x 100 = 300 186 x 3 = 558
18 + 240 + 300 = 558

1. 162 x 5 = 810
2. 398 x 2 = 796
3. 904 x 8 = 7,232
4. 329 x 5 = 1,645
5. 240 x 7 = 1,680
6. 432 x 6 = 2,592
7. 412 x 8 = 3,296
8. 542 x 9 = 4,878
9. 506 x 5 = 2,530
10. 554 x 6 = 3,324
11. 473 x 9 = 4,257
12. 257 x 8 = 2,056

Put commas in the following sentences to separate words in a series.

1. Nan, Tom, Julie, and James are going to a movie.
2. Anne took her spelling, reading, and math books to school.
3. The snack bar is only open on Monday, Tuesday, Friday, and Saturday.
4. Our new school flag is blue, green, yellow, black, and orange.
5. Women, men, children, and pets enjoy sledding.
6. Have you ever seen baby kittens, piglets, or goslings?
7. Carla and Mark bought postcards, film, candy, and souvenirs.

Now write four sentences of your own. Name at least three people, sports or foods in a series. Be sure to put in the commas.

8.–11. Answers will vary.

© Summer Bridge Activities™ 4-5 61 www.summerbrains.com

Page 61

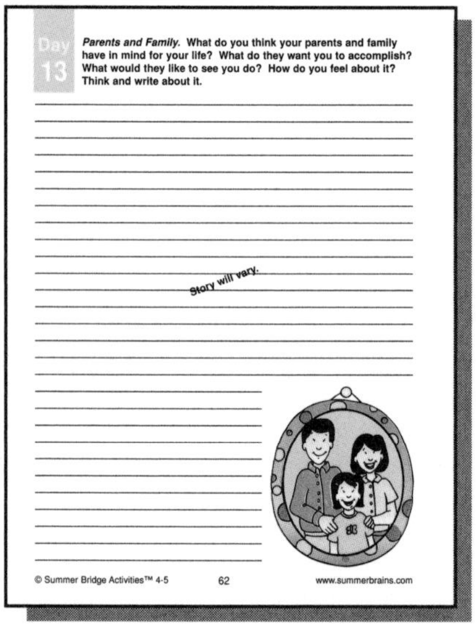

Parents and Family. What do you think your parents and family have in mind for your life? What do they want you to accomplish? What would they like to see you do? How do you feel about it? Think and write about it.

Story will vary.

© Summer Bridge Activities™ 4-5 62 www.summerbrains.com

Page 62

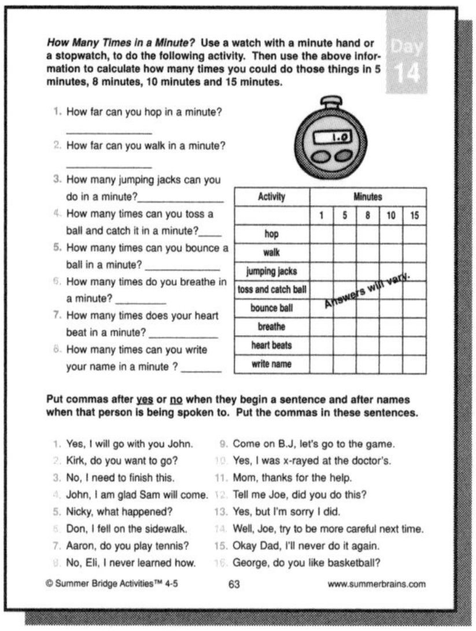

How Many Times in a Minute? Use a watch with a minute hand or a stopwatch, to do the following activity. Then use the above information to calculate how many times you could do those things in 5 minutes, 8 minutes, 10 minutes and 15 minutes.

1. How far can you hop in a minute?
2. How far can you walk in a minute?
3. How many jumping jacks can you do in a minute?
4. How many times can you toss a ball and catch it in a minute?
5. How many times can you bounce a ball in a minute?
6. How many times do you breathe in a minute?
7. How many times does your heart beat in a minute?
8. How many times can you write your name in a minute?

Activity	Minutes 1	5	8	10	15
hop					
walk					
jumping jacks					
toss and catch ball					
bounce ball					
breathe					
heart beats					
write name					

Answers will vary.

Put commas after yes or no when they begin a sentence and after names when that person is being spoken to. Put the commas in these sentences.

1. Yes, I will go with you John.
2. Kirk, do you want to go?
3. No, I need to finish this.
4. John, I am glad Sam will come.
5. Nicky, what happened?
6. Don, I fell on the sidewalk.
7. Aaron, do you play tennis?
8. No, Eli, I never learned how.
9. Come on B.J, let's go to the game.
10. Yes, I was x-rayed at the doctor's.
11. Mom, thanks for the help.
12. Tell me Joe, did you do this?
13. Yes, but I'm sorry I did.
14. Well, Joe, try to be more careful next time.
15. Okay Dad, I'll never do it again.
16. George, do you like basketball?

© Summer Bridge Activities™ 4-5 63 www.summerbrains.com

Page 63

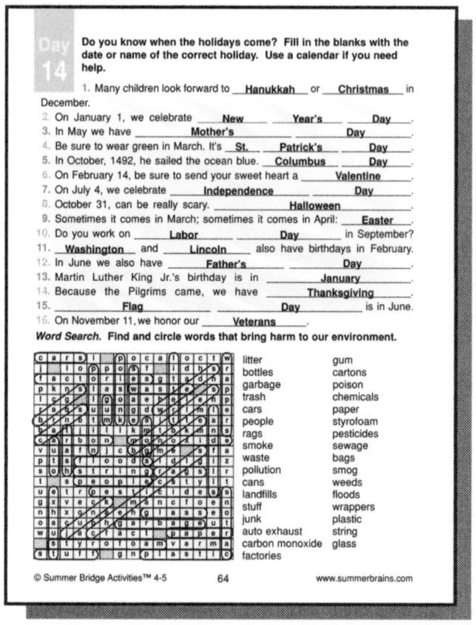

Do you know when the holidays come? Fill in the blanks with the date or name of the correct holiday. Use a calendar if you need help.

1. Many children look forward to Hanukkah or Christmas in December.
2. On January 1, we celebrate New Year's Day.
3. In May we have Mother's Day.
4. Be sure to wear green in March. It's St. Patrick's Day.
5. In October, 1492, he sailed the ocean blue. Columbus Day.
6. On February 14, be sure to send your sweet heart a Valentine.
7. On July 4, we celebrate Independence Day.
8. October 31, can be really scary. Halloween
9. Sometimes it comes in March; sometimes it comes in April: Easter.
10. Do you work on Labor Day in September?
11. Washington and Lincoln also have birthdays in February.
12. In June we also have Father's Day.
13. Martin Luther King Jr.'s birthday is in January.
14. Because the Pilgrims came, we have Thanksgiving.
15. Flag Day is in June.
16. On November 11, we honor our Veterans.

Word Search. Find and circle words that bring harm to our environment.

litter, bottles, garbage, trash, cars, people, rags, smoke, waste, pollution, cans, landfills, stuff, junk, auto exhaust, carbon monoxide, factories, gum, cartons, poison, chemicals, paper, styrofoam, pesticides, sewage, bags, smog, weeds, floods, wrappers, plastic, string, glass

© Summer Bridge Activities™ 4-5 64 www.summerbrains.com

Page 64

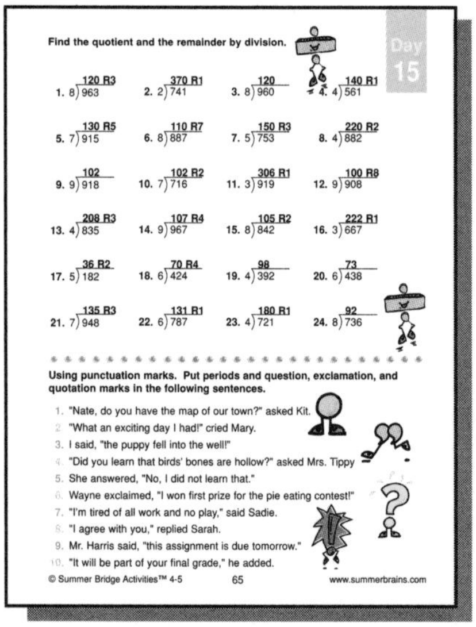

Find the quotient and the remainder by division.

1. 963 ÷ 8 = 120 R3
2. 741 ÷ 2 = 370 R1
3. 960 ÷ 8 = 120
4. 561 ÷ 4 = 140 R1
5. 915 ÷ 7 = 130 R5
6. 887 ÷ 8 = 110 R7
7. 753 ÷ 5 = 150 R3
8. 882 ÷ 4 = 220 R2
9. 918 ÷ 9 = 102
10. 716 ÷ 7 = 102 R2
11. 919 ÷ 3 = 306 R1
12. 908 ÷ 9 = 100 R8
13. 835 ÷ 4 = 208 R3
14. 967 ÷ 9 = 107 R4
15. 842 ÷ 8 = 105 R2
16. 667 ÷ 3 = 222 R1
17. 182 ÷ 5 = 36 R2
18. 424 ÷ 6 = 70 R4
19. 392 ÷ 4 = 98
20. 438 ÷ 6 = 73
21. 948 ÷ 7 = 135 R3
22. 787 ÷ 6 = 131 R1
23. 721 ÷ 4 = 180 R1
24. 736 ÷ 8 = 92

Using punctuation marks. Put periods and question, exclamation, and quotation marks in the following sentences.

1. "Nate, do you have the map of our town?" asked Kit.
2. "What an exciting day I had!" cried Mary.
3. I said, "the puppy fell into the well!"
4. "Did you learn that birds' bones are hollow?" asked Mrs. Tippy
5. She answered, "No, I did not learn that."
6. Wayne exclaimed, "I won first prize for the pie eating contest!"
7. "I'm tired of all work and no play," said Sadie.
8. "I agree with you," replied Sarah.
9. Mr. Harris said, "this assignment is due tomorrow."
10. "It will be part of your final grade," he added.

© Summer Bridge Activities™ 4-5 65 www.summerbrains.com

Page 65

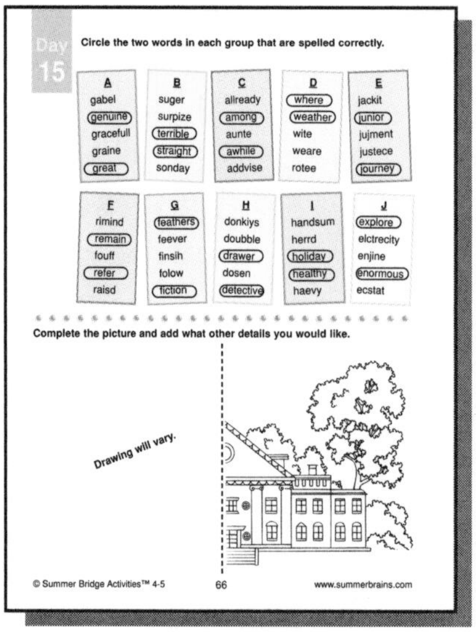

Circle the two words in each group that are spelled correctly.

A	B	C	D	E
gabel	suger	allready	(where)	jackit
(genuine)	surpize	(among)	(weather)	(junior)
gracefull	(terrible)	aunte	wite	jujment
graine	(straight)	(awhile)	weare	justece
(great)	sonday	addvise	rotee	(journey)

F	G	H	I	J
rimind	(feathers)	donkiys	handsum	(explore)
(remain)	feever	doubble	herrd	elctrecity
fouff	finsih	(drawer)	(holiday)	enjine
(refer)	folow	dosen	(healthy)	(enormous)
raisd	(fiction)	(detective)	haevy	ecstat

Complete the picture and add what other details you would like.

Drawing will vary.

© Summer Bridge Activities™ 4-5 66 www.summerbrains.com

Page 66

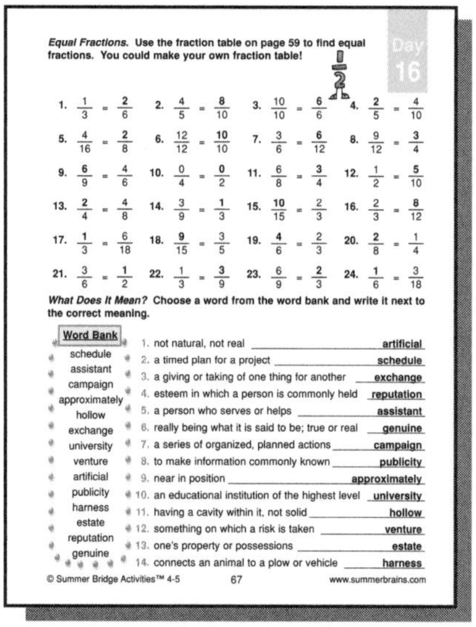

Equal Fractions. Use the fraction table on page 59 to find equal fractions. You could make your own fraction table!

1. $\frac{1}{3} = \frac{2}{6}$ 2. $\frac{4}{5} = \frac{8}{10}$ 3. $\frac{10}{10} = \frac{6}{6}$ 4. $\frac{2}{5} = \frac{4}{10}$
5. $\frac{4}{16} = \frac{2}{8}$ 6. $\frac{12}{12} = \frac{10}{10}$ 7. $\frac{3}{6} = \frac{6}{12}$ 8. $\frac{9}{12} = \frac{3}{4}$
9. $\frac{6}{9} = \frac{4}{6}$ 10. $\frac{0}{4} = \frac{0}{2}$ 11. $\frac{6}{8} = \frac{3}{4}$ 12. $\frac{1}{2} = \frac{5}{10}$
13. $\frac{2}{4} = \frac{4}{8}$ 14. $\frac{3}{9} = \frac{1}{3}$ 15. $\frac{10}{15} = \frac{2}{3}$ 16. $\frac{2}{3} = \frac{8}{12}$
17. $\frac{1}{3} = \frac{6}{18}$ 18. $\frac{9}{15} = \frac{3}{5}$ 19. $\frac{4}{6} = \frac{2}{3}$ 20. $\frac{2}{8} = \frac{1}{4}$
21. $\frac{3}{6} = \frac{1}{2}$ 22. $\frac{1}{3} = \frac{3}{9}$ 23. $\frac{6}{9} = \frac{2}{3}$ 24. $\frac{1}{6} = \frac{3}{18}$

What Does It Mean? Choose a word from the word bank and write it next to the correct meaning.

Word Bank: schedule, assistant, campaign, approximately, hollow, exchange, university, venture, artificial, publicity, harness, estate, reputation, genuine

1. not natural, not real artificial
2. a timed plan for a project schedule
3. a giving or taking of one thing for another exchange
4. esteem in which a person is commonly held reputation
5. a person who serves or helps assistant
6. really being what it is said to be; true or real genuine
7. a series of organized, planned actions campaign
8. to make information commonly known publicity
9. near in position approximately
10. an educational institution of the highest level university
11. having a cavity within it, not solid hollow
12. something on which a risk is taken venture
13. one's property or possessions estate
14. connects an animal to a plow or vehicle harness

© Summer Bridge Activities™ 4-5 67 www.summerbrains.com

Page 67

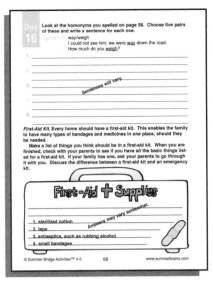

Day 16

Look at the homonyms you spelled on page 58. Choose five pairs of these and write a sentence for each one.

EXAMPLE: way/weigh
I could not see him; we were <u>way</u> down the road.
How much do you <u>weigh</u>?

1.
2.
3. Sentences will vary.
4.
5.

First-Aid Kit. **Every home should have a first-aid kit. This enables the family to have many types of bandages and medicines in one place, should they be needed.**

Make a list of things you think should be in a first-aid kit. When you are finished, check with your parents to see if you have all the basic things listed for a first-aid kit. If your family has one, ask your parents to go through it with you. Discuss the difference between a first-aid kit and an emergency kit.

First-Aid + Supplies

Answers may vary somewhat.

1. sterilized cotton
2. tape
3. antiseptics, such as rubbing alcohol
4. small bandages

© Summer Bridge Activities™ 4-5 68 www.summerbrains.com

Page 68

Adding Fractions. Day 17

$\frac{2}{3} + \frac{1}{3} = \frac{3}{3}$ ← add the numerator ← use the same denominator

1. $\frac{1}{3} + \frac{1}{3} = \frac{2}{3}$ 2. $\frac{1}{2} + \frac{1}{2} = \frac{2}{2}$ 3. $\frac{6}{12} + \frac{5}{12} = \frac{11}{12}$ 4. $\frac{6}{12} + \frac{7}{12} = \frac{13}{12}$

5. $\frac{5}{8} + \frac{2}{8} = \frac{7}{8}$ 6. $\frac{3}{10} + \frac{4}{10} = \frac{7}{10}$ 7. $\frac{1}{6} + \frac{2}{6} = \frac{3}{6}$ 8. $\frac{11}{12} + \frac{11}{12} = \frac{22}{12}$

9. $\frac{7}{10} + \frac{1}{10} = \frac{8}{10}$ 10. $\frac{1}{8} + \frac{6}{8} = \frac{7}{8}$ 11. $\frac{4}{9} + \frac{4}{9} = \frac{8}{9}$ 12. $\frac{7}{10} + \frac{6}{10} = \frac{13}{10}$

13. $\frac{1}{4} + \frac{2}{4} = \frac{3}{4}$ 14. $\frac{4}{10} + \frac{5}{10} = \frac{9}{10}$ 15. $\frac{3}{8} + \frac{3}{8} = \frac{6}{8}$ 16. $\frac{2}{8} + \frac{4}{8} = \frac{6}{8}$

17. $\frac{3}{6} + \frac{1}{6} = \frac{4}{6}$ 18. $\frac{4}{12} + \frac{5}{12} = \frac{9}{12}$ 19. $\frac{2}{8} + \frac{7}{8} = \frac{9}{8}$ 20. $\frac{8}{12} + \frac{5}{12} = \frac{13}{12}$

21. $\frac{3}{12} + \frac{8}{12} = \frac{11}{12}$ 22. $\frac{3}{10} + \frac{3}{10} = \frac{6}{10}$ 23. $\frac{5}{9} + \frac{5}{9} = \frac{10}{9}$ 24. $\frac{5}{8} + \frac{7}{8} = \frac{12}{8}$

Circle the abbreviations and titles in these sentences. <u>Remember:</u> Abbreviations are short forms of words and usually begin with capital letters and end with periods.

1. (Dr.) Cox is my family doctor.
2. Do you live on Rocksberry (Rd)?
3. My teacher's name is (Ms.) Hansen.
4. On (Mon). we are taking a trip to Salt Lake City, (Ut).
5. Will (Mr.) Harris sell his company to your parents?
6. Rick's birthday and mine are both on (Feb). 16.

Mister Fredrickson / Mr. Fredrickson

Now write the abbreviations for these words.

7. street	St.	13. Utah	Ut.
8. avenue	Ave.	14. Tuesday	Tues.
9. postscript	p.s.	15. Mister	Mr.
10. Miss	Ms.	16. tablespoon	Tbs.
11. January	Jan.	17. circle	Cir.
12. Thursday	Thurs.	18. company	Co.

© Summer Bridge Activities™ 4-5 69 www.summerbrains.com

Page 69

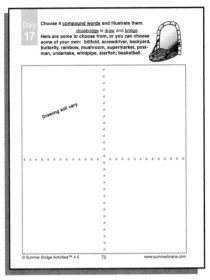

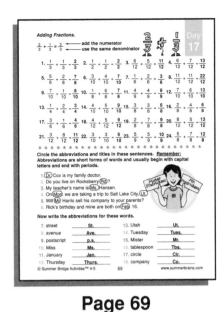

Day 17

Choose 4 <u>compound words</u> and illustrate them.

EXAMPLE: <u>drawbridge</u> is <u>draw</u> and <u>bridge</u>.

Here are some to choose from, or you can choose some of your own: billfold, screwdriver, backyard, butterfly, rainbow, mushroom, supermarket, postman, undertake, windpipe, starfish, basketball.

Drawing will vary.

© Summer Bridge Activities™ 4-5 70 www.summerbrains.com

Page 70

Understanding polygons. Day 18

Closed figures that have straight lines are *polygons*.
Which of these are polygons? 1,3,4,5

1. 2. 3. 4. 5.

Why? **<u>Because these all have straight lines and they are closed shapes.</u>**
Where each side or point meets is called a *vertex*. Count and write the number of sides and the number of vertices each polygon has.

	triangle	pentagon	quadrilateral	octagon
sides	3	5	4	6
vertices	3	5	4	6

How are these shapes below alike?
How are they different?

Write the book titles correctly. <u>Remember:</u> Underline the whole title and use capital letters at the beginning of all the important words and the last word in the title.

1. millions of cats — <u>Millions of Cats</u>
2. higher than the arrow — <u>Higher than the Arrow</u>
3. john paul jones — <u>John Paul Jones</u>
4. no flying in the house — <u>No Flying in the House</u>
5. ludo and the star horse — <u>Ludo and the Star Horse</u>
6. marvin k. money, will you please leave now? — <u>Marvin K. Money, Will You Please Leave Now?</u>
7. an elephant is not a cat — <u>An Elephant is Not a Cat</u>
8. one wide river to cross — <u>One Wide River to Cross</u>
9. the polar express — <u>The Polar Express</u>
10. where the sidewalk ends — <u>Where the Sidewalk Ends</u>

© Summer Bridge Activities™ 4-5 71 www.summerbrains.com

Page 71

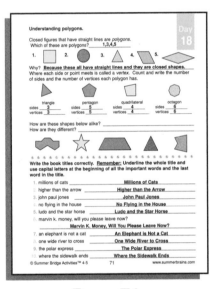

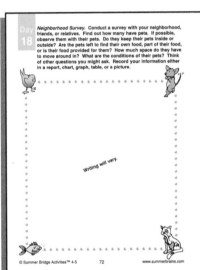

Day 18

Neighborhood Survey. **Conduct a survey with your neighborhood, friends, or relatives. Find out how many have pets. If possible, observe them with their pets. Do they keep their pets inside or outside? Are the pets left to find their own food, part of their food, or is their food provided for them? How much space do they have to move around in? What are the conditions of their pets? Think of other questions you might ask. Record your information either in a report, chart, graph, table, or a picture.**

Writing will vary.

© Summer Bridge Activities™ 4-5 72 www.summerbrains.com

Page 72

Use what you know about polygons to make a pattern. Start with one polygon and flip, turn, or slide it to make a pattern. Day 19

EXAMPLE:

or

Now try your hand at making some polygon patterns.

Drawing will vary.

Review of Homonyms or Homophones. **Write 10 sentences using some of these pairs of homonyms or homophones. Be sure to use both words and underline the homonyms you use.**

EXAMPLE: <u>Would</u> you chop some <u>wood</u>?

1. no, know	7. sun, son	13. rode, road
2. ate, eight	8. tail, tale	14. pair, pear
3. see, sea	9. sell, sail	15. their, there
4. knight, night	10. so, sew	16. hour, our
5. new, knew	11. way, weigh	17. red, read
6. four, for	12. sent, cent	18. wear, where

Sentences will vary.

Here are some examples:
1. I am going to <u>sell</u> my <u>sailboat</u>.
2. I <u>knew</u> I needed to practice the <u>new</u> words.
3. <u>Their</u> house is over <u>there</u>.
4. <u>Where</u> is the shirt I'm going to <u>wear</u>?
5. <u>No</u>, I don't <u>know</u> how to ride a bike!

© Summer Bridge Activities™ 4-5 73 www.summerbrains.com

Page 73

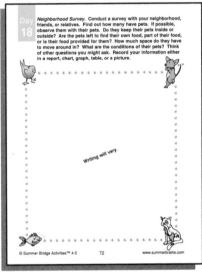

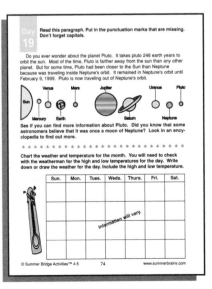

Day 19

Read this paragraph. Put in the punctuation marks that are missing. Don't forget capitals.

Do you ever wonder about the planet Pluto. It takes pluto 248 earth years to orbit the sun. Most of the time, Pluto is farther away from the sun than any other planet. But for some time, Pluto had been closer to the Sun than Neptune because was traveling inside Neptune's orbit. It remained in Neptune's orbit until February 9, 1999. Pluto is now traveling out of Neptune's orbit.

Sun, Mercury, Venus, Earth, Mars, Jupiter, Saturn, Uranus, Neptune, Pluto

See if you can find more information about Pluto. Did you know that some astronomers believe that it was once a moon of Neptune? Look in an encyclopedia to find out more.

Chart the weather and temperature for the month. You will need to check with the weatherman for the high and low temperatures for the day. Write down or draw the weather for the day. Include the high and low temperature.

Sun.	Mon.	Tues.	Weds.	Thurs.	Fri.	Sat.
			Information will vary.			

© Summer Bridge Activities™ 4-5 74 www.summerbrains.com

Page 74

Rename these fractions. The first one is done for you. Day 20

1. $\frac{5}{4} = 1\frac{1}{4}$ 2. $\frac{10}{3} = 3\frac{1}{3}$ 3. $\frac{9}{8} = 1\frac{1}{8}$ 4. $\frac{8}{3} = 2\frac{2}{3}$

5. $\frac{5}{2} = 2\frac{1}{2}$ 6. $\frac{7}{4} = 1\frac{3}{4}$ 7. $\frac{10}{3} = 3\frac{1}{3}$ 8. $\frac{11}{10} = 1\frac{1}{10}$

9. $\frac{10}{7} = 1\frac{3}{7}$ 10. $\frac{19}{8} = 2\frac{3}{8}$ 11. $\frac{25}{10} = 2\frac{5}{10}$ 12. $\frac{9}{5} = 1\frac{4}{5}$

13. $\frac{31}{10} = 3\frac{1}{10}$ 14. $\frac{23}{10} = 2\frac{3}{10}$ 15. $\frac{17}{8} = 2\frac{1}{8}$ 16. $\frac{13}{3} = 4\frac{1}{3}$

17. $\frac{25}{12} = 2\frac{1}{12}$ 18. $\frac{28}{9} = 3\frac{1}{9}$ 19. $\frac{36}{10} = 3\frac{6}{10}$ 20. $\frac{9}{4} = 2\frac{1}{4}$

21. $\frac{13}{6} = 2\frac{1}{6}$ 22. $\frac{215}{100} = 2\frac{15}{100}$ 23. $\frac{76}{25} = 3\frac{1}{25}$ 24. $\frac{100}{3} = 33\frac{1}{3}$

Name the parts of a letter.

1. Heading
2. Greeting
3. Body
4. Closing
5. Signature

1624 Oak Avenue
Amarillo, TX 79103
June 20, 1995

Dear Patt,

Today my friends and I went swimming in June's pool. We had a lot of fun.

I sure miss you. I wish your family hadn't moved. Have you made any new friends yet?

Please write to me as soon as you can.

Your friend,
Judy

© Summer Bridge Activities™ 4-5 75 www.summerbrains.com

Page 75

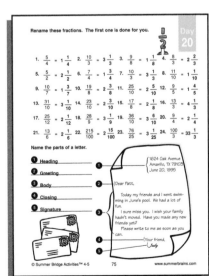

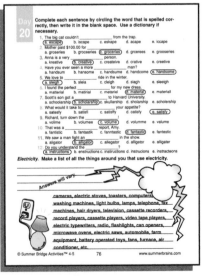

Day 20

Complete each sentence by circling the word that is spelled correctly, then write it in the blank space. Use a dictionary if necessary.

1. The big cat couldn't ______ from the trap.
   (a. escape) b. iscape c. eskape d. acape e. iccape
2. Mother paid $100.00 for ______.
   a. groseries b. groceeries (c. groceries) d. grcerees e. grooseries
3. Anna is a very ______ person.
   a. kreative (b. creative) c. createive d. crative e. creetive
4. Have you ever seen a more ______ man?
   a. handsum b. hansome c. handsume d. handcome (e. handsome)
5. We love to ______ ride in the winter.
   (a. sleigh) b. sleia c. cleigh d. slagh e. sleeigh
6. I found the perfect ______ for my new dress.
   a. matterial b. matirial c. metariel (d. material) e. materiall
7. Scott's son got a ______ to Harvard University.
   a. schoolarship (b. scholarship) c. skullarship d. sholarship e. scholership
8. What would it take to ______ your appetite?
   a. satesfy b. satisfi c. satisffy d. catisfy (e. satisfy)
9. Richard, turn down the ______!
   a. volime b. volumee (c. volume) d. volumme e. valume
10. That was a ______ report, Amy.
   a. fantistic b. fantastik c. fanntastic (d. fantastic) e. fantestic
11. We saw a man fight an ______ in the show.
   a. aligator (b. alligator) c. allegator d. alligetor e. alligater
12. Do you understand the ______?
   (a. instructions) b. enstructions c. insitructions d. instrucions e. instracteons

Electricity. **Make a list of all the things around you that use electricity.**

Answers will vary.

cameras, electric stoves, toasters, computers, washing machines, light bulbs, lamps, telephone, fax machines, hair dryers, television, cassette recorders, record players, cassette players, video tape players, electric typewriters, radio, flashlights, can openers, microwave ovens, electric saws, automobile, farm equipment, battery operated toys, fans, furnace, air conditioner, etc.

© Summer Bridge Activities™ 4-5 76 www.summerbrains.com

Page 76

Section 3

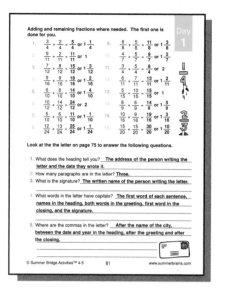

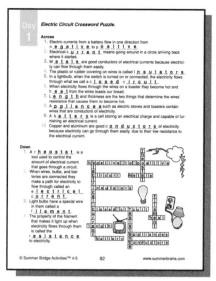

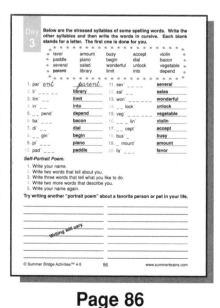

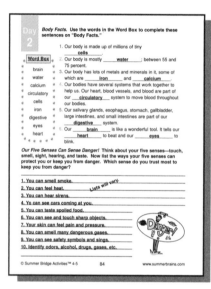

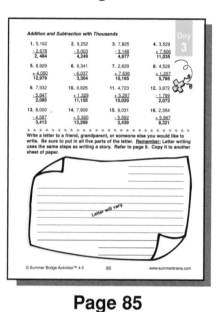

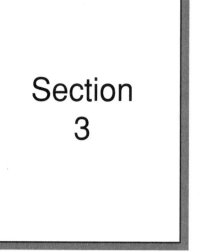

Page 86

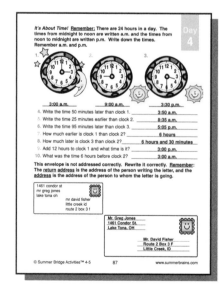

Page 87

Page 88

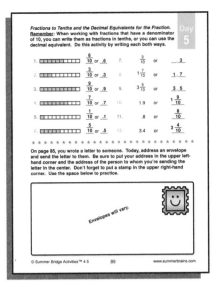

Page 89

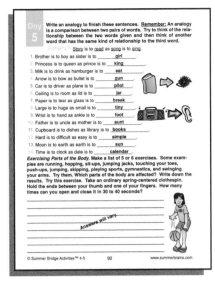

Page 90

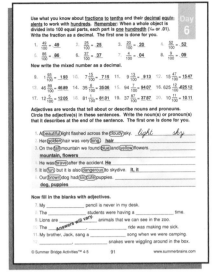

Page 91

Page 92

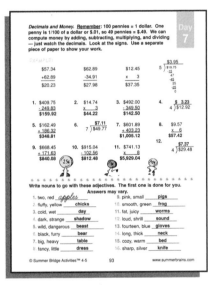

Page 93

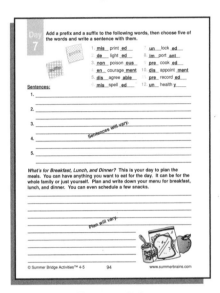

Page 94

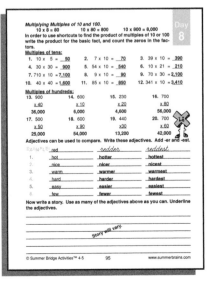

Page 95

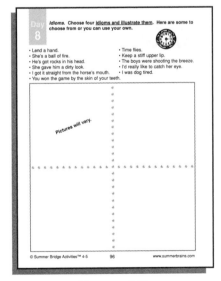

Page 96

Page 97

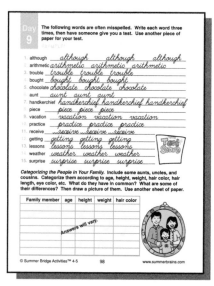

Page 98

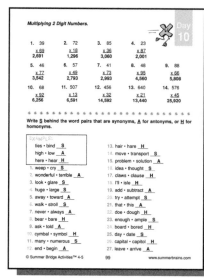

Page 99

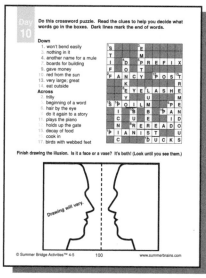

Page 100

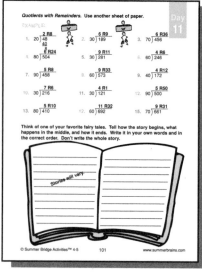

Page 101

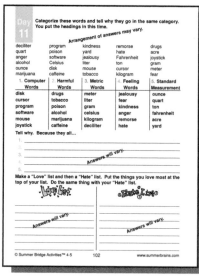

Page 102

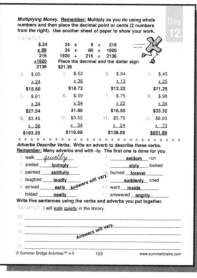

Page 103

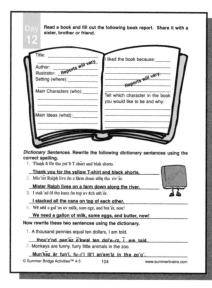

Page 104

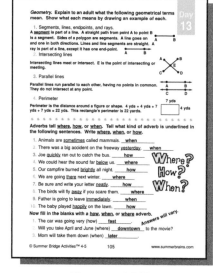

Page 105

Page 106

Page 107

Day 14

More Geometry. Explain and draw an example of the following geometrical terms.

1. **Congruent figures** are polygons that have the exact shape and size. The can be flipped, slid or turned, but as long as they are the exact shape and size they are congruent.

2. **Right angles** are angles that form a square corner. All of these are right angles. When two lines form 4 right angles, we say that the are perpendicular.

These are congruent figures.
These are right angles.

3. **Triangles** have three sides and 3 vertices (vertex). Vertex is where the points meet.

sides — vertex

4. **Parallelograms** are four-sided figures having the opposite sides parallel and equal.

5. **Polygons** are closed, straight sided figures. Triangles, hexagons, octagons, pentagons, and quadrilaterals are all polygons. This is also a polygon because it is a closed figure with straight lines.

Sometimes it's fun to share a story with someone else. Read a book, then call one of your friends or go visit them. Tell your friend about the book you read.

Tell who the main characters are. Tell where the story takes place. Tell the plot–main event of the story. But don't tell them how the story ends. See if you can get them to read the book.

On the rest of the page, write what happened. Did you get your friend to read the book?

Answers will vary.

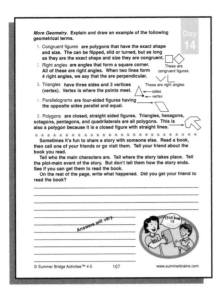

© Summer Bridge Activities™ 4-5   107   www.summerbrains.com

Page 108

Day 14

Create small words from letters in the following words. Write them. You may find more than one in most words.

EXAMPLE: borrow *row* or *bow* *rob*

1. pajamas **jam, am, as, a**
2. carpenter **car, pen, enter**
3. performance **perform, for, man**
4. bandage **band, and, age, ban, an**
5. knowledge **know, no, now, ledge**
6. theory **the, or, he**
7. satisfaction **sat, is, fact, act, at, action**
8. customer **us, Tom, custom**
9. discovery **is, cover, very**
10. eventually **even, all, vent**
11. announcement **an, no, men, cement, announce, noun, Ann, ounce**
12. sentence **sent, ten**
13. theater **the, he, eat, ate**
14. honorable **honor, on, or, able**
15. investigate **in, vest, gate, ate, invest**

Sometimes things happen that cause something else to happen. This is called "cause and effect." A clue word helps to tell which is which. In the following sentences, underline the cause with a straight line (___). Underline the effect with a dotted line (_ _ _). Put a box ☐ around the clue word. The first one is done for you.

1. The tooth was broken, ☐so☐ it gave her a lot of pain.
2. The book was ripped and dirty ☐because☐ the dog got it.
3. ☐Because☐ it was so cold, Betty could ice skate for only a short while.
4. I went to bed early last night ☐because☐ I was so tired.
5. ☐Since☐ it was raining so hard, we couldn't play outside.
6. The rabbit ran fast ☐because☐ the fox was after it.
7. It was very foggy out, ☐so☐ we could not see the mountains.
8. ☐Because☐ we got to the camp late in the day, there was no time for hiking.
9. It was very dark in the dugout ☐so☐ we turned on the flashlight.
10. Kit played basketball too long after school, ☐therefore☐ he missed the bus.
11. Laura's letter was returned ☐because☐ she forgot to put a stamp on it.
12. Mike's suitcase broke when it fell off the car. ☐As a result☐ he had to put his things in a paper bag.

© Summer Bridge Activities™ 4-5   108   www.summerbrains.com

Page 109

Day 15

Graphs, Charts, and Tables. There are many different kinds of graphs, charts, and tables. Check your newspaper regularly to find different kinds and different information that you could chart or graph daily. This is a "broken-line" graph. Complete this graph using the information given in the table. Monday and Tuesday have been done for you.

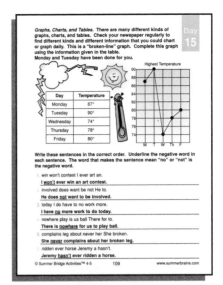

Day	Temperature
Monday	87°
Tuesday	90°
Wednesday	74°
Thursday	78°
Friday	80°

Highest Temperature

Write these sentences in the correct order. Underline the negative word in each sentence. The word that makes the sentence mean "no" or "not" is the negative word.

1. win won't contest I ever art an.
   I won't ever win an art contest.
2. involved does want be not He to.
   He does not want to be involved.
3. today I do have to no more work.
   I have no more work to do today.
4. nowhere play is us ball There for to.
   There is nowhere for us to play ball.
5. complains leg about never her She broken.
   She never complains about her broken leg.
6. ridden ever horse Jeremy a hasn't.
   Jeremy hasn't ever ridden a horse.

© Summer Bridge Activities™ 4-5   109   www.summerbrains.com

Page 110

Day 15

Match the definitions below to a word in the word box. Find and circle the words in the puzzle. The first one has been done for you.

1. ABC order
2. not a vowel
3. more than one
4. names things
5. mark used for stress
6. part of a word
7. describes nouns
8. used in place of a noun
9. added to the beginning of a base word
10. just one
11. describes verbs
12. not a consonant
13. added to the end of a base word
14. shows action

Word Box

- 12 vowel
- 3 plural
- 6 syllable
- 1 alphabetical
- 2 consonant
- 9 prefix
- 7 adjectives
- 4 nouns
- 14 verb
- 13 suffix
- 8 pronoun
- 11 adverbs
- 5 accent
- 10 singular

© Summer Bridge Activities™ 4-5   110   www.summerbrains.com

Multiplication and Division

Developing multiplication and division math skills can be a challenging experience for both parent and child.

- **Have a positive attitude.**
- **Relax and enjoy the learning process.**
- **Keep the learning time short and fun you will get better results.**
- **Review the cards with your child.**
- **Read the front of the card.**
- **Check your answer on the reverse side.**
- **Separate those he/she does not know.**
- **Review those he/she does know.**
- **Gradually work through the other cards.**

These steps will help build your child's confidence with multiplication and division. Enjoy the rewards!

● ●

"Teacher, Teacher"

Three or more players.
Each player takes a turn as "Teacher."
The Teacher mixes up the flashcards and holds one card up at a time.
First player to yell out "Teacher, Teacher,"
will have the first chance to give the answer.
If his/her answer is right he/she receives 5 points.
If his/her answer is wrong, he/she will not receive any points.
Move on to the next person until someone answers correctly.
The next round someone else is teacher.
Repeat each round.
Reward the different levels, everyone wins!

Time Challenge

Follow the directions for "Teacher, Teacher" and add a time to it.
Increase the point system to meet the Time Challenge.
Reward the different levels, everyone wins!

0 x 0	0 x 1	0 x 2	0 x 3
4	3	2	1
0 x 4	0 x 5	0 x 6	0 x 7
8	7	6	5
0 x 8	0 x 9	0 x 10	1 x 1
12	11	10	9

$1\overline{)1}$

0

$1\overline{)2}$

0

$1\overline{)3}$

0

$1\overline{)4}$

0

$1\overline{)5}$

0

$1\overline{)6}$

0

$1\overline{)7}$

0

$1\overline{)8}$

0

$1\overline{)9}$

1

$1\overline{)10}$

0

$1\overline{)11}$

0

$1\overline{)12}$

0

2 x 1	2 x 2	3 x 1	3 x 2
4	3	2	1
3 x 3	4 x 1	4 x 2	4 x 3
8	7	6	5
4 x 4	5 x 1	5 x 2	5 x 3
12	11	10	9

$2\overline{)2}$

6

$2\overline{)4}$

3

$2\overline{)6}$

4

$2\overline{)8}$

2

$2\overline{)10}$

12

$2\overline{)12}$

8

$2\overline{)14}$

4

$2\overline{)16}$

9

$2\overline{)18}$

15

$2\overline{)20}$

10

$2\overline{)22}$

5

$2\overline{)24}$

16

5 x 4	5 x 5	6 x 1	6 x 2
4	3	2	1
6 x 3	6 x 4	6 x 5	6 x 6
8	7	6	5
7 x 1	7 x 2	7 x 3	7 x 4
12	11	10	9

$3\overline{)3}$	$3\overline{)6}$	$3\overline{)9}$	$3\overline{)12}$
12	6	25	20
$3\overline{)15}$	$3\overline{)18}$	$3\overline{)21}$	$3\overline{)24}$
36	30	24	18
$3\overline{)27}$	$3\overline{)30}$	$3\overline{)33}$	$3\overline{)36}$
28	21	14	7

$\begin{array}{r} 7 \\ \times\,5 \\ \hline \end{array}$	$\begin{array}{r} 7 \\ \times\,6 \\ \hline \end{array}$	$\begin{array}{r} 7 \\ \times\,7 \\ \hline \end{array}$	$\begin{array}{r} 8 \\ \times\,1 \\ \hline \end{array}$
4	3	2	1
$\begin{array}{r} 8 \\ \times\,2 \\ \hline \end{array}$	$\begin{array}{r} 8 \\ \times\,3 \\ \hline \end{array}$	$\begin{array}{r} 8 \\ \times\,4 \\ \hline \end{array}$	$\begin{array}{r} 8 \\ \times\,5 \\ \hline \end{array}$
8	7	6	5
$\begin{array}{r} 8 \\ \times\,6 \\ \hline \end{array}$	$\begin{array}{r} 8 \\ \times\,7 \\ \hline \end{array}$	$\begin{array}{r} 8 \\ \times\,8 \\ \hline \end{array}$	$\begin{array}{r} 9 \\ \times\,1 \\ \hline \end{array}$
12	11	10	9

$4\overline{)4}$

8

$4\overline{)8}$

49

$4\overline{)12}$

42

$4\overline{)16}$

35

$4\overline{)20}$

40

$4\overline{)24}$

32

$4\overline{)28}$

24

$4\overline{)32}$

16

$4\overline{)36}$

9

$4\overline{)40}$

64

$4\overline{)44}$

56

$4\overline{)48}$

48

9 x 2	9 x 3	9 x 4	9 x 5
4	3	2	1
9 x 6	9 x 7	9 x 8	9 x 9
8	7	6	5
10 x 1	10 x 2	10 x 3	10 x 4
12	11	10	9

$5\overline{)5}$

45

$5\overline{)10}$

36

$5\overline{)15}$

27

$5\overline{)20}$

18

$5\overline{)25}$

81

$5\overline{)30}$

72

$5\overline{)35}$

63

$5\overline{)40}$

54

$5\overline{)45}$

40

$5\overline{)50}$

30

$5\overline{)55}$

20

$5\overline{)60}$

10

10 x 5 4	10 x 6 3	10 x 7 2	10 x 8 1
10 x 9 8	10 x10 7	11 x 1 6	11 x 2 5
11 x 3 12	11 x 4 11	11 x 5 10	11 x 6 9

$6 \overline{)6}$

80

$6 \overline{)12}$

70

$6 \overline{)18}$

60

$6 \overline{)24}$

50

$6 \overline{)30}$

22

$6 \overline{)36}$

11

$6 \overline{)42}$

100

$6 \overline{)48}$

90

$6 \overline{)54}$

66

$6 \overline{)60}$

55

$6 \overline{)66}$

44

$6 \overline{)72}$

33

11 x 7 4	11 x 8 3	11 x 9 2	11 x10 1
11 x11 8	0 x11 7	12 x 1 6	12 x 2 5
12 x 3 12	12 x 4 11	12 x 5 10	12 x 6 9

$7 \overline{)7}$	$7 \overline{)14}$	$7 \overline{)21}$	$7 \overline{)28}$
110	99	88	77
$7 \overline{)35}$	$7 \overline{)42}$	$7 \overline{)49}$	$7 \overline{)56}$
24	12	0	121
$7 \overline{)63}$	$7 \overline{)70}$	$7 \overline{)77}$	$7 \overline{)84}$
72	60	48	36

12 x 7	12 x 8	12 x 9	12 x 10
9	8	7	6
12 x11	12 x12	12 x 0	8)8
1	12	11	10
8)16	8)24	8)32	8)40
5	4	3	2

$8\overline{)48}$

120

$8\overline{)56}$

108

$8\overline{)64}$

96

$8\overline{)72}$

84

$8\overline{)80}$

1

$8\overline{)88}$

0

$8\overline{)96}$

144

$9\overline{)9}$

132

$9\overline{)18}$

5

$9\overline{)27}$

4

$9\overline{)36}$

3

$9\overline{)45}$

2

$9\overline{)54}$

9

$9\overline{)63}$

8

$9\overline{)72}$

7

$9\overline{)81}$

6

$9\overline{)90}$

1

$9\overline{)99}$

12

$9\overline{)108}$

11

$10\overline{)10}$

10

$10\overline{)20}$

5

$10\overline{)30}$

4

$10\overline{)40}$

3

$10\overline{)50}$

2

$10\overline{)60}$

9

$10\overline{)70}$

8

$10\overline{)80}$

7

$10\overline{)90}$

6

$10\overline{)100}$

1

$10\overline{)110}$

12

$10\overline{)120}$

11

$11\overline{)11}$

10

$11\overline{)22}$

5

$11\overline{)33}$

4

$11\overline{)44}$

3

$11\overline{)55}$

2

$11\overline{)66}$ $11\overline{)77}$ $11\overline{)88}$ $11\overline{)99}$

9   8   7   6

$11\overline{)110}$ $11\overline{)121}$ $11\overline{)132}$ $12\overline{)12}$

0   12   11   10

$12\overline{)24}$ $12\overline{)36}$ $12\overline{)48}$ $12\overline{)60}$

0   0   0   0

$12\overline{)72}$

9

$12\overline{)84}$

8

$12\overline{)96}$

7

$12\overline{)108}$

6

$12\overline{)120}$

1

$12\overline{)132}$

12

$12\overline{)144}$

11

$2\overline{)0}$

10

$4\overline{)0}$

5

$6\overline{)0}$

4

$9\overline{)0}$

3

$11\overline{)0}$

2

Certificate
of
Completion

Awarded to

_____

for the completion of Summer Bridge Activities™
4th grade to 5th grade.

_____
Ms. Hansen
Ms. Hansen

_____
Mr. Fredrickson
Mr. Fredrickson

Parent's Signature

Place
Proper
Postage
Here

SKYHAWKS
PO Box 18529
Spokane, WA 99228-0529

Sports Programs for Kids • Sports Programs for Kids • Sports Programs for Kids

Place
Proper
Postage
Here

Rainbow Bridge Publishing
PO Box 571470
Salt Lake City, Utah 84157

Your Summer Education Specialists • Keeping Children Busy, Happy & Learning